Soccer
Memorabilia

A Collectors' Guide

Graham Budd

Philip Wilson Publishers

First published in 2000 by
Philip Wilson Publishers Ltd
143-149 Great Portland Street
London W1N 5FB

Distributed in the USA and Canada by
Antique Collector's Club
91 Market Street Industrial Park
Wappingers' Falls
New York 12590

ISBN 0 85667 504 0

Edited by Antony Wood
Designed by Andrew Shoolbred

Printed and bound in Italy by
Società Editoriale Lloyd, Srl, Trieste

Contents

Overleaf
Guillermo Laborde (1886–1940)
The official poster of the 1930 World Cup

5

For Françoise

Acknowledgements

The publishers and I would like to thank all those museums, companies, dealers, private collectors and other individuals who permitted their works to be reproduced in this book.

I am grateful to Sotheby's for allowing me to use their photographic archives and for the arrangement of special photography. Special thanks are extended to Heath Cooper, Paul Brickell and Danny Deudney in this respect.

I am especially grateful to Bryan Horsnell, Norman Shiel, David King, Ian Wright, Sean Arnold, Phil Martin, Roy Calmels, John Eastwood and Ceri Stennett for their practical help and enthusiastic support during the production of this book.

I would like to thank Cangy Venables at Philip Wilson Publishers and my agent Mary Martinez for all their hard work during this project. My greatest thanks, however, are for my wife Françoise, whose love, support and practical assistance made this book possible.

Picture Acknowledgements

Numbers refer to plates

Sotheby's London 3–4, 14–16, 19, 22, 26, 34–36, 40–43, 45–46, 51, 53–54, 57, 59–60, 62–63, 66, 70–82, 87–94, 99, 103
Private Collections 1–2, 17, 97
Bryan Horsnell Collection 5–6, 8–12, 18, 20–21, 27–28, 39, 55, 64–65
Manchester United Football Club Museum 7, 96, 98
Liverpool Football Club Museum 13
The Football Museum, Preston 24
Sean Arnold Sporting Antiques, London 25
Ian Wright (sports memorabilia consultant and soccer historian), France 29–33, 47–50, 52, 56, 58, 95
Sainsbury's 61
Phil Martin Collection 83–86
Wilkinson Sword Limited 100
Nestlé UK Ltd & Sotheby's 101
Electronic Arts (Sports) 102

Introduction

Soccer is without question the most popular sport in the world. At the highest level today, the game has transcended the parameters of a sporting pursuit and has evolved into a complex, multibillion-dollar global business, with a myriad of political, social and economic implications. It is difficult to foresee a time when soccer will fail to retain the extraordinary spell that it holds over millions of people throughout the world.

The origins of the game remain lost in antiquity, although there is evidence suggesting that a type of ball game was played in China and the East, and in ancient Greece and Rome. Soccer as we know it today, however, has its historical roots very firmly planted in the British Isles. It was the inauguration of the Football Association in 1863 (with the Scottish Football Association formed ten years later) that initiated the whole evolutionary process; for it was their crucial unifying influence and proper administration that allowed the game to flourish in an orderly manner. In a short space of time, the sport was refined, organised and finally exported all around the globe.

With this rich and proud past it seems incredible that the first museums devoted to British soccer heritage on a national scale are only now opening their doors to the public. It must be hoped that the proposed Scottish Football Museum at Hampden Park, and the Football Museum at Preston will provide a much deserved and long overdue gravitas to this important area of British sporting and social history.

Writing 40 years ago in a volume entitled *Association Football* (published by Caxton), Geoffrey Green, journalist and author, observed: 'The curse of the twentieth century is that more and more there is less time for looking back. The accent is on the immediate present and perhaps the immediate future. That is what it has become ... As millions watch their football, do many of them, I wonder, ever look back, or even want to look back? How did the business of chasing a ball around a strip of grass and trying to force it between uprights at each end, ever come about? Where did it start? How long has it been going on? What was it like in the dim past? Does it all, in fact, matter? Of course it does. Because if we know a little about the past it helps sometimes to explain the present.'

At the beginning of a new century and a new millennium, some of the above author's fears can be allayed. The tide has clearly turned and many devotees of the game have become passionately interested in soccer's fascinating story. As Geoffrey Green reminds us, soccer, or for that matter any subject, can become a far more rewarding experience when witnessed in the light of

Previous page
Autographs and examples of the means by which they can be collected.

history. A striking example of this over last decade or so has been the tremendous surge of interest in soccer memorabilia. For many, simply following the game is no longer enough. There is now a need to become closer to the teams and individuals, matches and events, incidents and developments that have shaped and enriched the sport's history. Collectors derive great satisfaction from acquiring material related to the game they love, helping the pages of the history book come to life in a vivid and tangible form.

The result has been a growth of auction house sales devoted to, or containing, items of soccer memorabilia and a marked increase in the number of dealers and trade fairs specialising in the subject. Much material is readily available to the public throughout the calendar, a situation in marked contrast to the experience of the small nucleus of collectors who foresaw the importance and value of soccer heritage in earlier times. Today the activity is also well supported by the various collectors clubs and publications that have sprung up, offering advice, information and news to new and experienced collectors alike.

The 1990s were an overwhelming success story for British soccer at its highest levels. The nation now boasts some of the finest stadiums in the world, and unimaginable riches have flowed into the game since the inauguration of the FA Premier League in 1992, helping clubs to finance the acquisition of some of the world's finest players. During the decade the English national team were a penalty shoot-out away from the final of a World Cup and a European Championship, the latter evoking tremendous interest in the sport as the nation hosted Euro '96. Sell-out crowds are now a common occurrence in the Premier League. Soccer's renaissance as the foremost national sport has been truly remarkable and far reaching.

It is surely not chance that this youthful area of collecting has coincided with the current boom experienced by the game itself. Conversely, it may be because of the opulence of the modern game that many have grown more curious about the past. Perhaps they have become nostalgic over older, less complicated times, a golden era when magnificent players from the clubs they support turned out week after week for little financial reward. It is perhaps this true affection for soccer that fans can relate to so closely, and the heroics of admired individuals that collectors are most interested in celebrating and preserving.

A vast range of memorabilia is available to the collector, and the decision of what to collect is typically an evolutionary process rather than a calculated game plan from the outset. Many indeed prefer to collect items of an eclectic nature, focusing on material that has a particular meaning for the individual, or which strikes a chord with their own sense of soccer history. Others may concentrate on a specific category of memorabilia or amass material relating directly to the club they support. Often the seeds of a collecting tendency may have been sewn at an early age. For many years supporters' shops at clubs have presented collectables for sale, and now merchandise has mushroomed into a lucrative alternative source of income for many clubs. There can be few fans who have not kept at least some match programmes for games they attended, or have not obtained a player's autograph or two along the way. It is often from the small beginnings like this that authoritative collections grow.

The aim of this book is to show the diversity of soccer memorabilia now available, illustrating and discussing artefacts on a category by category basis. At the end of the book some addresses of institutions and organisations are provided where soccer memorabilia may be seen and acquired, and from which collectors can seek further help, advice and information.

Soccer memorabilia is a fascinating field of collecting, soundly based on the mass popularity of the sport, and affording a huge amount of pleasure. The infectious enthusiasm of collectors whom I've had the pleasure to meet has certainly rubbed off on me, and if this book plays any part in adding to their number, then it will have been a success.

Football Association Challenge Cup match at the Kennington Oval: Blackburn Rovers v. Notts County: coloured print, signed W.D.A.

chapter one

Caps

A long tradition in professional and amateur British soccer has been to honour a player involved in an international or representative game by the award of a cap. Indeed, the word 'cap' has become synonymous with an appearance by a player for the national side. More interestingly, the term has entered the international language of the game. It would not be surprising to hear a German commentator, for example, describing the national team's goalkeeper as 'winning his fiftieth cap', even though there is no such tradition in Germany, or for that matter anywhere outside the United Kingdom and the Republic of Ireland.

The tradition has also evolved in amateur international soccer, and caps have also been awarded by the various regional Football Associations for representative appearances, as well as by other institutions such as the armed forces for inter-services games. Caps are presented for both codes of international rugby; while the cricket authorities have developed their own awards system for capping cricketers at county and test levels. The public schools and universities also have a long tradition of awarding caps to players in a variety of sports.

The symbolism of a cap as a choice of award arises from the fact that footballers wore a cap as part of their uniform during the game's formative years. Moreover, the cap was the primary method of distinguishing the two teams on the field of play before sides began wearing distinctive coloured jerseys. Caps were a means by which individual players could be identified by spectators, long before the advent of numbered shirts. Some early printed match cards, forerunners of the modern soccer programme, have details of the team line-ups accompanied by the colour of cap that the player would be wearing during the match. On some occasions the identification extended to the colour of stockings that were to be worn as well. Caps were only abandoned as a regular part of a player's attire when heading became a prevalent practice. The exception to this was the goalkeeper, who was not required to wear a colour of jersey distinct from his outfield colleagues, and the cap remained the means by which he was identified during play.

Caps are amongst the most highly prized items of soccer memorabilia for collectors, especially international caps connected to the cream of players from a generation. The decorativeness and colour of caps enhances their appeal to the collector. They also form a subject that is poorly recorded in official records, and part of their fascination for collectors has been that they are testimony to a clearer picture of soccer history. One by one, missing

1 England international caps awarded to Roy Goodall of Huddersfield Town (left to right): A maroon and white England v. France international cap, 1927; a black, red and orange England v. Germany international cap, 1930; a green and red England v. Italy international cap, 1933; a purple and orange England v. Belgium international cap, 1931; and a black and maroon England v. Austria international cap, 1932–33.

pieces of the jigsaw have been slotted into place as caps from different eras and different countries have appeared on the auction market and expertise in reading them has consolidated and grown accordingly.

The birthplace of international soccer is a matter of some debate, but the match between Scotland and England at the West of Scotland Cricket Club, Hamilton Crescent, Glasgow on the 30 November 1872 is now generally recognised as having been the first official international soccer match in the world. A famous print of this match shows both sides wearing caps, with the Scottish side wearing an extraordinary form of headgear resembling an old-fashioned gentlemen's nightcap. Between 1876 and 1882 Wales and Ireland appeared on the international scene, and from 1884 the four nations began playing an annual round of matches against each other that became known as the Home International Championship. This tradition endured for precisely one hundred years, before it was finally abandoned in 1984 because of an increasingly congested international fixture list and also the blight of hooliganism. Outside the United Kingdom official international soccer match did not exist until 1 May 1904, the date of the historic encounter between France and Belgium.

The first official England international caps were awarded in 1886 at the suggestion of Mr N. Lane ('Pa') Jackson, one of the most enthusiastic legislators at the Football Association, and an important figure in the England team's early international history. In 1882 Jackson had founded the legendary Corinthians Football Club, the most famous and romantic name in amateur football.

The earliest England international caps were royal blue in colour and embellished with a rose motif. At first these were awarded only to players for the Scotland match, but when the Home Championship matches became established, the English Football Association adopted a system of awarding differently coloured caps (2), according to the opposition. For an appearance against Scotland a purple cap was presented, maroon against Wales, and white against Ireland. Each still retained the embroidered rose emblem, and the year of the match was embroidered on the peak.

To these three basic designs of cap must be added the international trial cap, awarded to footballers who played in specially arranged matches where their ability could be assessed by international selectors. Typically such a match may have been billed as 'Probables v. Possibles'. The trial cap was designed with eight alternating purple and white panels, with the rose emblem replaced by a white embroidered FA monogram.

The Football Association maintained this colour-coded system for matches against the home nations, and then expanded the concept in response to the greater internationalisation of soccer. This process began with England's match against Austria in Vienna on 6 June 1908, the first

2 England international caps awarded to Roy Goodall of Huddersfield Town (left to right): A purple England v. Scotland international cap, 1927–28; a purple and white Football Association international trial cap, 1927–28; a white England v. Ireland international cap, 1932–33; and a maroon England v. Wales international cap, 1932–33.

fully recognised international game between a British side and an overseas side. What followed was the most interesting and certainly the most colourful period of cap manufacture (1). As England played a foreign side for the first time, different alternating panels of colour were employed for the cap's design. The same colour combination would be used again should the sides meet in subsequent internationals. These highly decorative caps hold a particular appeal for collectors, especially when a new colour combination surfaces for the first time.

Just before the Second World War, in the 1938–39 season, the colour coding system appears to have been abandoned. By 1938 England had played a total of fifteen overseas teams, and already combinations of three colours were being used to identify the opposition on caps. Some colours had also been reserved for caps awarded to players who took part in the various Football Association tours, such as those of Australia and South Africa in the 1920s. It seems plausible to suggest that the Football Association may have found that the system was becoming unwieldy, and foresaw a time when the England cap would resemble that of a harlequin's costume, as international soccer continued to expand. In the immediate future, of course, world events were to intervene and curtail any such developments on the soccer field.

In place of the coloured caps, including the home international variations, a plain cap was introduced (3), blue-purple with an embroidered match inscription on the peak to identify the game. The rose emblem was also replaced by the Football Association's famous 'three lions' crest embroidered in gilt-metal wire work. This emblem of a vertical column of lions within a shield and surmounted by a crown is very similar to the design of the cloth badge that had been emblazoned on English players' jerseys since the very first international in 1872.

This particular style of England cap was to prove unique to the 1938–39 season. Although there were a number of wartime international matches, they were not deemed to be official games and no caps were awarded. When full international soccer did resume in the 1946–47 season, a new design of cap appeared. It was now dark blue with the three lions embroidered in white above the inscription The Football Association, which like the match inscription on the peak was in a Gothic-style script.

In the post-war era the England cap evolved through a number of stylistic changes. Silver-white piping was introduced to the cap, forming six distinct panels, while similar braiding encompassed the rim of the cap and its peak, and a decorative tassel was suspended from beneath a button finial at the crown of the cap, at the point where the piping of the panels converged. In the 1949–50 season the Football Association inscription disappeared, and the three lions emblem settled into the format recognisable to us today, with the blue lions interspersed with ten red roses within a white shield. This was a result of an official Grant of Arms being issued to the Football Association by the Royal College of Arms. In 1950 the cap became larger and baggier, and its colour lightened and settled as a plush mid-blue (4), having fluctuated between dark and mid-blue hues during the late 1940s. The Gothic-style match inscription remained in place, although it varied a good deal between issues. Examples include a full match inscription of both teams; just the name of the opposition, sometimes preceded by a v or E v (England versus); or just the initials of the opposing teams, for example E v I (England v. Italy). The date of the inscription also varies between the year and the season of the match.

Another significant change in the post-war era was the issuing of a combined cap by the FA. This began with the Home International Championships, and a player received just a single cap, even if he had played in two or the full three games of the competition. The initials of the opposition were embroidered onto the one, common cap. This system later extended to other multi-gamed tournaments and to summer tours. Eight of the eleven England players in the victorious 1966 World Cup winning side played in all six matches during the tournament. Each, however, received a single cap inscribed World Championship, Jules Rimet Cup, 1966, with the names of the opposing sides embroidered on the six panels into which the cap was divided. It may thus be seen that the number of caps a player actually received often does not at all equate with the number of his recorded appearances.

That said, the number of opportunities to win caps since the war has been incomparably greater than in earlier times. Four England players – Billy Wright, Sir Bobby Charlton, Bobby Moore and Peter Shilton – have all performed the outstanding achievement of winning over one hundred caps. With far fewer international matches taking place before the war, a career total of between twenty and thirty caps would also represent a magnificent achievement for the period.

Another feature of modern times has been the structure of the various intermediate England teams, acting as a nursery ground for possible future

3 A blue England v. Wales international cap, 1938–39, awarded to Walter Boyes of West Bromwich Albion. This design of cap is unique to the 1938–39 season.

internationalists, who compete in such matches as schoolboy and youth internationals. These players are also presented with caps by the Football Association, which can roughly be likened to the tradition of the old international trial caps.

Moving on to the caps of the other home nations and the Republic of Ireland (5), the first point to notice is that the basic designs of the Scottish, Welsh and Irish caps have always been very similar to the format eventually adopted by England after much historical meandering. The crest of the inidividual Football Association, with decoration such as braiding, tassels and match inscriptions, often formed the fundamental design of these nations' caps from a very early stage.

The most significant difference between the Football Associations has lain in their awarding policies. The Scottish Football Association only began presenting caps to players for appearances in the Home International Championship. From 1929 Scotland began playing overseas sides in international matches, commencing with the game against Norway in Bergen on 26 May, but no caps were awarded for these matches, and if a Scottish player's only appearances for the national side happened to be against foreign teams, then he would have gained no caps at all. This policy continued until the 1970s, when the Scottish FA began awarding a single cap covering all appearances by a player during an international season, with no match inscriptions on the cap. Accordingly, many Scottish internationalists received no more than a single cap a season, although they may have played in a large number of matches. From about 1992 the Scottish FA began awarding caps for individual games.

The Scotland cap was manufactured in a number of colours before the First World War, but not it would seem as a means of identifying the opposition. The dark blue of the Scotland jersey has always been the predominant colour, although red was used on a number of occasions in the early part of the twentieth century, whilst other known variations include purple-blue and pale pink. All were embellished with gilt-metal wire decoration, with the decorative tassel present on many early examples and becoming a perennial feature. The crest of the Scottish Football Association – a rampant lion within a shield surrounded by thistle – is embroidered on the cap, and above it can be found the match inscription, usually the initials of the opponents, for example S v. E (Scotland v. England). The date of the match is embroidered on the peak.

The cap's colour settled at blue during the inter-war period, with some variation, although always in a rich or dark shade. Stylistically there was little change until the 1970s when gilt-metal piping formed six distinctive panels on the cap, the design of the Scottish FA crest underwent several revisions, and specific match inscriptions disappeared during the seasonal cap period.

4 A blue England v. Italy international cap, 1952–53, awarded to Billy Wright of Wolverhampton Wanderers.

The Football Association of Wales has always awarded caps to players on a seasonal basis. An amusing exception to this rule was the legendary Welsh internationalist Billy Meredith who also ran a sportswear outfitters business, which held the franchise with the Welsh FA at the turn of the century to manufacture the caps. Consequently, he was allowed to produce his own personal caps representing specific matches, some of which are unique in colour and design.

The seasonal caps were effectively a combined cap for appearances in the Home International Championships, with the exception of seasons 1932–33 and 1938–39, when Wales played matches against France, their only games against overseas opposition before the War. After the resumption of international soccer, Welsh caps began to bear match inscriptions with the initials of the opposition, home nations or otherwise. From season 1971–72, these inscriptions were abandoned, as the increase in international fixtures had made the practice too complicated and had led to a number of erroneous issues to players.

The earliest Welsh international caps date from about 1890 and were green in colour with a rampant dragon emblem, although caps designed with alternating black and white panels were awarded in the latter part of this decade. By 1900 the cap had settled as green and was decorated with the red Welsh Dragon emblem, beneath the inscription FAW (Football Association of Wales), with the year of the match on the peak. During the Edwardian era the cap began to be embellished with piping and a tassel. A gold tassel was used for senior team matches, while a silver tassel denoted an amateur international and a red tassel a junior game. This design was largely unaltered until the Second World War, although a special red cap was produced on the occasion of the first encounter with France in 1933, which has naturally become a collector's item. Match inscriptions also changed in the late 1920s from the year of the match to that of the international season.

From 1946–47 the colour of the Welsh cap was changed to burgundy red on a permanent basis, with the dragon emblem becoming gold and matching the remainder of the decoration including the peak's match inscriptions. In season 1951–52, and to celebrate the 75th anniversary of the Welsh FA, the Royal College of Arms awarded a special crest. The dragon emblem was now enclosed by a shield above a Welsh inscription that translates as 'Team Play is the Best Play', and the new crest appeared on caps and jerseys. From 1972–73 it was manufactured as a fully coloured emblem, as opposed to being picked out in different coloured threads.

The Irish Football Association is the fourth oldest in the world, and Ireland played their first game against England in 1882. The Irish FA should not be confused with the Football Association of Ireland, who have been governing the game in Eire since political partition in 1923. The original Association continued its participation in the Home International Championships, after this date fielding the team under the new name of Northern Ireland. The Republic of Ireland entered the international scene in the Olympic Games of 1924 in Paris, recording a 1-0 win in the first game against Bulgaria.

The caps presented by the earlier Irish Football Association have been on a seasonal basis most of the time, and have been remarkably consistent in their design. They are blue in colour with the gilt-metal decoration typical of the examples previously discussed. Specific match inscriptions, in the form of the initials of opponents, have been found on known examples in the 1960s. The early crest of the Irish Football Association incorporated a central shamrock, and was later redesigned as an inscribed Celtic cross and circle motif.

Caps for the players of the Republic of Ireland have always been green in colour, divided by gilt-metal decoration into panels in the normal way, and embellished with tassels. Pre-war examples bear a crest of the Irish Free State, which appears to have disappeared when international soccer resumed. They were always awarded seasonally and usually bear full match inscriptions denoting Ireland and the name of the opponents, and where the match was played. However, from the 1970s onwards, opponent's names have been omitted from the design. The season is embroidered on the peak, with the number of matches played indicated by a figure in a reserved shield design on the front panel of the cap.

chapter two

Medals

6 Top (left to right)
Bury FC medals from season
1902–03:
Commemorative medal awarded
to players when they won the
1903 FA Cup final by a record
score of 6-0 against Derby
County. They did not concede a
single goal in the competition
The reverse of William Wood's FA
Cup winner's medal; and Bury FC
commemorative medal recording
their 1903 treble of the FA Cup,
Lancashire Cup and Manchester
and District Cup.

Centre (left to right):
1947 FA Cup final linesman's
medal, awarded by the Football
Association; 1950 FA Cup final
referee's medal, awarded by the
Football Association; and 1950
FA Cup final referee's commemorative medal, awarded by the
Referees' Association.

Bottom (left to right):
An official's lapel badge from the
1911 FA Cup final; FA Charity
Shield winner's medal,
Newcastle United, 1909; and FA
Cup runners-up medal,
Newcastle United, 1911.

It has often been said that sport acts as a pacific substitute for war. Certainly the language of sport mirrors the battlefield, with talk of tactics, strategies, offence and defence, victories and defeats. This analogy would seem to extend to the choice of medals for the decoration of sportsmen, with its echoes of the Orders of Gallantry won by the brave and courageous in times of battle.

The trophy was first by far the most usual prize for sporting winners, but the award of medals became more prevalent with the introduction of team games, especially soccer, in the second half of the nineteenth century. While the winning team would be presented with a trophy, it was also necessary to recognise each individual's contribution in a suitably commemorative manner.

Medals are the most cherished items for footballers, and are enduring evidence of a successful career. Even today, with the vast financial awards available, the dream and ambition of every player to win medals remains undiminished. Because of their highly personal and evocative nature and a direct connection with successful players and their achievements, medals are amongst the most prestigious items of soccer memorabilia.

It is simply not known when the first soccer medals were presented. But it is clear that the tradition of prize medals in soccer was in place from an early stage, and that it pervaded virtually every level of the game from the highest professional ranks to the humblest local or junior competition. Consequently, a huge number of medals have little meaning or importance other than being a cherished family item or of local historical interest. A comprehensive examination of soccer medals at all levels could occupy the entire pages of a book in its own right, and so this chapter will concentrate on a selection of medals that have significant interest and are connected with prestigious competitions. We begin with the Football Association Challenge Cup.

The competition was the brainchild of Charles William Alcock, an Old Harrovian who was still a player with Wanderers (and who would play in the first final of 1872 in which Wanderers beat the Royal Engineers) when he proposed the competition to the FA Committee on 20 July 1871. After slight vacillation, the committee agreed to the idea and a set of eighteen rules for the competition were drafted on 16 October. Here there is a specific reference to the trophy and the awarding of medals. Rule 13 states: 'The holders of the Challenge Cup shall hand it over to the Secretary of the Football Association on or before 1st February in each year, unless the holders shall have won the Cup three years in succession, when the Cup shall become the absolute property of the Club so winning it. In addition to the Cup, the committee will present to the winners of the Final Tie, eleven medals or badges, of trifling value.' The cautious description of the medals' value is no doubt a response to the amateur status of players at this period, reflecting wariness of any criticism that this first important soccer competition may have become exposed to.

At present, no FA Cup winner's medal is known to exist from a date earlier than 1876 (in a private collection), the fifth year of the competition, also then won by Wanderers. The preceding period is therefore still obscure, and we cannot be sure in what exact form these original Victorian trifles, alluded to in the FA rules, were manufactured.

The 1876 medal was in the form of a small gold disc, the obverse struck with a segmented football in raised relief encircled by a laurel wreath, the classical symbol of victory. In the 1880s the medals were made of a high quality 22-carat gold before they were completely redesigned in season 1894–95. Now in 15-carat gold, the new medal (7) was struck with two footballers wearing baggy shirts with the sleeves rolled up and long knickerbockers, cut beneath the knee; beneath the Royal Standard is a scrolling panel reserved for the date to be engraved. When the medals were presented immediately after the final tie, they were given in an uninscribed state. It was up to the club or the player to arrange for the medal to be inscribed with the winner's name and details of the match on the reverse of the medal. Consequently, a number of entirely uninscribed medals are in existence where this action was never taken. The only clues to the occasion under these circumstances is the year stamp of the gold hallmark and family provenance.

This winner's medal with the Geminean-style footballers has remained the classic design ever since, although there have been several modifications to the medal over the years, with the purity and weight of the gold also reduced. In 1933, for example, the purity of the gold was reduced from 15 to 14-carat and remained so until the war.

Between 1940 and 1945, with many players serving overseas, the FA Cup competition was suspended. Petrol shortages and the general difficulties of public travel at this period made soccer hard to stage, but a series of unofficial and regionalised FA Cup-type tournaments were organised by the Football League. Medals made from 9-carat gold were presented in season 1939–40, but the practice had to be abandoned for the remainder of the war, and players received savings certificates instead. There is some evidence that the winning clubs themselves may have commissioned unofficial medals to commemorate their achievements, a known example being a bronze medal

7 FA Cup winner's medal, 1909, won by Dick Duckworth of Manchester United. From the collection of the Manchester United Museum.

commissioned by Preston North End following their defeat of Arsenal in the 1941 War Cup final.

With the resumption of the FA Cup proper in 1946, but with gold in scarce supply, bronze medals were originally awarded. However, the FA subsequently arranged for 9-carat gold medals to be presented retrospectively, made in the normal design. The purity of the gold has remained at 9-carat ever since.

Quite soon after the war the dress of the two footballers depicted on the medal was revised and updated. The players now wore more fitted shirts with an open collar, and shorts cut above the knee, in keeping with the changing times. The Royal Standard was also replaced by the Football Association's Three Lions crest. There has been little change stylistically to the present day.

It is not known precisely when runners-up medals were first introduced for FA Cup finalists, but it is generally believed to have been sometime in the mid-1890s, possibly in conjunction with the new style of winner's medal. The 9-carat gold medal (6) once again featured the Royal Standard, this time surmounted by a crown. Surrounding the Standard are three botanical emblems of the Union – the thistle of Scotland, the shamrock of Ireland and the rose of England. At the base of the medal is a segmented football in raised relief, beneath a Football Association inscription.

After the Second World War the runners-up medal was redesigned. It now featured a player leaping to head a panelled football, while to the right a second player looks on beyond. The base of the medal was struck with a central Three Lions shield, with rose and laurel wreath motifs either side.

Perhaps a lesser known fact is that the three match officials also receive medals (6) from the Football Association for their roles in the final, an event that often represents the crowning achievement of their own particular sporting careers. The examples illustrated are from 1947 and 1950 (6). Referees can also receive commemorative medals from the Referees' Association.

The story of the Scottish Football Association Cup begins in 1873, when fifteen clubs subscribed towards the purchase of the cup. The trophy and medals are recorded at a cost of £56 12s 11d. The famous amateur side Queen's Park, who had also entered the English competition in its formative years, won the first final played at Hampden Park, Glasgow, on 21 March 1874.

The original Scottish Cup medals of 1874 were in the form of a silver cross, but there followed a period of annual redesigns before they finally settled at a basic, enduring design from season 1888–89. Although it has passed through a number of subtle stylistic revisions over the years, the Scottish 9-carat gold and enamel winners' medal (8) took the form of a central open-work rampant lion enclosed by a circular band inscribed in

enamel Scottish Football Association, and with the lower curve of the band designed as a buckle. The medal's suspension was formed as a stylised thistle.

During the 1890s the purity of the gold was increased to 15-carat, before reverting to the original specification after the Great War. In 1932 it was increased once more, this time to 14-carat before finally settling at 9-carat after the Second World War.

On 17 April 1888 a group met at an old coaching inn in Manchester's Piccadilly at the suggestion of Mr William McGregor of Aston Villa FC, a Birmingham shopkeeper. His proposal was to organise a series of regular fixtures throughout the season. From this meeting the Football League was born, with its twelve original members contesting the first soccer competition of its kind in the world.

The early Championship winning medals were commissioned by the clubs themselves (9), and therefore display a great deal of individual variation from year to year. The clubs often chose to incorporate their crests on the enamel work of the gold medal, or alternatively they were at least enamelled in the club's colours. On other occasions the medals were struck with traditional laurel wreath motifs, or with representations of the Football League trophy, and sometimes lacked any enamelling.

After the Great War the medals were presented officially by the Football

8 Left to right: 1912 Scottish League Championship medal, Rangers FC; 1920 Scottish League Championship medal, Rangers FC; and 1899 Scottish FA Cup winner's medal, Celtic FC.

League (10) and took on the classic appearance that was to endure until very recent times, before finally showing variance with the medals presented at the advent of Football League commercial sponsorship. The 9-carat gold Football League medal incorporated a near centre football in raised relief surrounded by laurel wreaths, beneath a reserved panel inscribed The Football League. Beneath the football and laurel there were two further scrolling panels, in which were inscribed Champions and, for example, Division 1. The historical development of the Football League divisions as they expanded, regionalised and deregionalised over the years means that six variations of these medals were produced, namely Divisions One, Two, Three

9 Top (left to right): Newcastle United FC, Division One League Champions medal, 1906–07; and Glossop North End FC, medal commemorating promotion to Division One of the Football League, 1898–99.

Centre (left to right): Aston Villa FC, Football League Champions' medal, 1896–97; 1918–19 Football League War Fund medal, Stoke v. Leeds City; and Aston Villa FC medal commemorating the 1896–97 Cup and League double.

Bottom (left to right) Inter-League medals: Southern League v. Scottish League and Irish League medal, 1913; Scottish League v. Southern League medal, 1914–15; and Football League v. Irish League, 1901.

(Southern Section), Three (Northern Section), Three and Four.

For a period following the Second World War, and with gold in scarce supply, the lower league medals were manufactured in silver gilt before reverting to the normal 9-carat gold.

In the late 1970s the Football League began awarding gold plaques (12) set in wooden surrounds instead of traditional gold medals. These did not prove popular with players, and by the early 1980s the Football League had reverted to the presentation of traditional medals.

Over the years clubs have commissioned their own unofficial medals to commemorate the achievements of their players – for example, if a club gained promotion to the First Division (9). Aston Villa commissioned a commemorative medal when they won the 'double' in season 1896–97 (9). Bury FC also commissioned special medals for their highly successful 1902–03 season (6).

The Scottish League was formed on 30 April 1890 and was based on the English model, with eleven founder members. The arguments of professionalism were still rumbling on in Scotland at this period, and unlike their English counterparts the Scottish sides contesting the first League Championship of 1890–91 were still bound to a strict amateur status.

The medals for the Scottish League Championships are remarkable for their lack of conformity. At first glance one might believe that a new design was chosen at the beginning of each season, but a closer examination reveals that some medals did endure for brief periods, while other examples are the result of a previous design being revisited and revised. Nevertheless, there are countless different examples in existence, which makes for a particularly varied field of collecting (8).

10 The six variations of the Football League Championship medal:
(Top, left to right) Division One, Two and Three.

(Bottom, left to right) Division Four, Three (Southern Section) and Three (Northern Section.)

11
(Top, left to right)
A Football Association international medal, 1927
A 1919 England v. Scotland Victory International medal, 1919.

(Bottom, left to right)
FA Amateur Cup winner's (1908) and runners-up (1898) medals.

Scottish Championship medals are usually manufactured in 9-carat gold and enamel, although there are occasional examples in 15-carat gold, and at certain periods, especially the 1920s and 1930s, enamelling was abandoned. Variations of designs include cross shapes, circular or oval medals with SFA or city crests, open-work circular laurel wreaths, and many others. Similar variations of design extended to the medals awarded to the championships of the lower Scottish divisions.

Running in parallel to the Home International Championships for many years were the Inter-League fixtures, contested by the Football League and their counterparts in Scotland and Ireland. The first such game that has been officially recognised took place on 11 April 1892 at Pike's Lane, Bolton (then the ground of Bolton Wanderers), between the Football League and the Scottish League. In this fixture the Football League fielded four Scots who were playing professionally in England at this time. However, the League quickly assumed a policy of selecting only English players and adhered to this with very few exceptions until the policy was finally reversed in the 1950s.

12 Football League Division Two championship plaque, given in lieu of medals in 1978; and an FA Charity Shield plaque, given to both winners and losers in 1992.

The Southern League also played a total of thirty-three fixtures between 1910 and 1981, while the League of Ireland joined the scene from the Republic in 1939, and the Italian League added a genuinely international flavour to proceedings after the war. The Football League finally abandoned Inter-League fixtures in 1976.

The Football League, the Scottish League and the Southern League all awarded medals (9) for appearances in these fixtures, and the English examples from the late Victorian period display some variation. There are star-shaped medals manufactured in gold with a central enamelled Three Lions shield, while circular and other shaped medals display traditional heraldic symbols such as crowns and lions, and the Union emblems of thistle and shamrock, depending on the opposition, usually in relief on the gold, but sometimes within enamelled crests. The purity varies between 9-carat and 15-carat gold.

The Football League medals, however, soon assumed a design that was kept until the eventual demise of the fixtures. This consisted of a 9-carat gold oval-shaped medal with a central football in raised relief, surrounded by the rose of England and either thistle or shamrock. Around this central design was a Football League inscription and a specifically engraved match inscription, the latter replaced after the Second World War by an all encompassing version simply worded Representative Match. At this period the medal was also degraded from the original gold specification to silver gilt.

The Scottish Inter-League medals vary in design between those that incorporate traditional home nation crests and examples that look similar to the Scottish FA Cup medal, with the central open-work rampant lion. Later, a circular 9-carat gold and enamel medal was employed, with a central Rampant Lion crest surmounted by a crown and surrounded by thistle. After the Second World War, enamelling disappeared and a plain 9-carat gold medal struck with a thistle in raised relief was presented to the participating players.

In addition to the caps awarded to players for appearances in international matches, the Football Association, during the inter-war years, also provided England players with an opportunity to receive a commemorative medal (11) to mark their international début. The internationalist was given the option of receiving his match fee in the normal manner or forsaking the money in favour of the medal presentation. The 14-carat gold medal was struck with a classical figure standing behind the Royal Standard with both arms outstretched and clutching laurel wreaths, while to either side of the Standard can be seen two footballs in raised relief.

13 A selection of medals won by Kenny Dalglish on display in the Liverpool Football Club Museum: including two European Cup winner's medals, and a gold and enamel Milk Cup winner's medal, 1984. European domestic competitions began in the 1950s and became an increasingly important target for clubs sides. Today, the UEFA Champions League has become established as the ultimate goal for major European clubs.

The Football Association Charity Shield was founded in 1908, the match being contested between Manchester United, the Football League Champions, and Queen's Park Rangers, the Southern League Champions. The competition directly replaced the Sheriff of London Shield, which had been played annually between 1898 and 1907.

Although the general rule has been to pitch the best two sides in the country together for the occasion, there were many deviations from this principle before the game transferred to Wembley Stadium in 1975. From this point onwards, the match has been contested between the English League and Cup winners (double-winning seasons excepted).

The medals for the Charity Shield (6) were originally circular shaped with a central Three Lions shield, and the gold appears to have fluctuated between 9 and 14-carat, but normally the latter. After the Second World War the presentation of a commemorative plaque was introduced. Originally the plaque was manufactured in an attractive classical design in silvered metal with an enamelled Three Lions crest, and mounted onto an oak panel backboard with an easel support. In the early 1950s, however, it was somewhat downgraded and now consisted of a silvered medallion (12) of the FA Crest set into a black octagonal bakelite backboard.

Another traditional Wembley showpiece was the Football Association Amateur Challenge Cup final (from 1949 to 1974), which allowed amateur players to experience the thrill of playing an important match beneath the shadows of the stadium's famous Twin Towers. Medals were awarded to winners and runners-up (11). The competition is in fact a great deal older, and was first contested at Richmond in 1894 with Old Carthusians defeating Casuals 2-1. Its eventual demise in 1974 was caused when the Football Association deemed the term 'amateur' no longer to have any significant meaning.

14 The glittering prize! A continental gold World Cup winner's medal awarded to Schubert Gambetta of Uruguay, 1950.

chapter three

Kit and Equipment

When Pelé described soccer as the Beautiful Game, he was also alluding to the pure simplicity of the activity. It is an exciting, free-flowing sport and not overburdened with complicated or technical rules. Its simplicity also extends to the equipment that is used, which in comparison to many other sports is fairly basic and inexpensive. This helps explain why the game's popularity has grown so immediately wherever it has been introduced.

Visual records of early soccer matches reveal that the basic principles of a player's dress and equipment have changed little over the years. Styles may have changed from jerseys, knickerbockers and stockings, to shirts, shorts and socks, materials and their technological manufacture may have been revolutionised, but the functionality of soccer is remarkably similar to the original concepts. This is true of many sports, for example seventeenth-century prints of jockeys depict them in silks, breeches and peaked caps and they are immediately recognisable characters to the modern eye.

Perhaps the most striking new aspect of the modern soccer jersey is not its design, but the way it acts as a moving advertisement hoarding for the sportswear manufacturer and for the club's commercial sponsors. Add to this the modern phenomenon of the replica jersey, and it appears that the whole crowd attending the match is achieving the same objectives, fulfilling a marketeer's wildest dreams.

The only provisions in the rules of the game relating to dress state, in Law IV: 'the basic compulsory equipment of a player shall consist of a jersey or shirt, shorts, stockings, shin-guards and footwear ... a player shall not wear anything which is dangerous to another player ... the goalkeeper shall wear colours which will distinguish him from the other players and the referee.'

In the early days of grass roots soccer, the demand from players and clubs was for inexpensive, basic clothing from local suppliers. If this could not be found then they were more than content to don lightweight trousers and ordinary working shirts and boots. This often led to a good deal of nonconformity of dress within the team, and as discussed in a previous chapter, it was primarily the colour of cap that would unite the players. A contemporary account of a match in Darwen in the late 1870s noted: 'One or two of the Darwen team wore long cloth trousers, with braces over a dark shirt. Those who boasted knickerbockers, had these useful garments made from old trousers cut down. Their shirts were of all kinds, and two of their prominent players wore sweaters.'

Many of the grander amateur clubs, on the other hand, copied the ideas

15 FA Cup final shirts and jerseys dating between 1907 and 1991:
Harry Burton's blue and white striped Sheffield Wednesday shirt (1907); William Watson's claret and blue Burnley jersey (1914); Lionel Smith's red; and white Arsenal shirt (1952) and Nayim's white Tottenham Hotspur jersey, 1991.

of the public schools and adopted specifically coloured soccer uniforms. Some of the weird and wonderful concoctions from the period include Horncastle, Lincs (1861), white trousers, light blue socks, blue belt and cap with gold tassel, white shirt with blue facings; Sheffield Mackenzie (1862), plaid cap with pink shirt; Royal Engineers (1863), jersey, nightcap and stockings of blue and red in horizontal stripes, and dark knickerbockers; and Black Rovers, Hackney (1869), black jersey with white skull and cross-bones on breast, black cap and stockings, and white knickerbockers.

In their early days, it was not unusual for clubs to change the colour of their strips quite frequently, sometimes from season to season. It was only when something approaching a tradition had been established that teams began sticking with what had become the acknowledged team colours. Supporters became increasingly proud of their club colours and it was the foremost way by which fans could identify their own particular allegiance. Club nicknames began to arise from the team colours, such as the 'Blues' and 'Reds', and attempts to change this tradition were likely to have been met with fervent opposition. The most common cause of colour changes appears to be based on superstition. There are many recorded instances of clubs hoping to change their luck by adopting a new-coloured shirt, especially from green which was thought to be especially unlucky and explains why so few British sides play in this particular colour.

As well as becoming traditionalist, clubs also became more conservative in their choice of jerseys. Many of the more exotic colour combinations and style of markings, such as sashes, multi-coloured stripes and hoops, halves and quarters and even spotted shirts, were abandoned with very few exceptions (the Blackburn Rovers' halves being one such example) in favour of plainer one- or two-colour body and sleeve designs.

Many of the first players' jerseys were made of a thick, knitted wool, but cotton often proved cheaper and more practical. From this period they often look more like rugby shirts, especially with their thick cuffs and button-up collars, with the vogue being for baggy, loose-fitting shirts and shorts. *The Complete Association Footballer* (Methuen & Co. Ltd, 1912) is the earliest comprehensive literary work on the theory and practice of soccer, and sheds fascinating light on the game at this period. It advises on dress as follows: 'The shorts worn (also shirt) should be very loose and easy, particularly across the hips. It is impossible to play in a pair of knickers that fit like one's skin. If a belt is worn, care should be taken that the buckle does not rest on the

16 A woollen England international shirt, c.1925, Tommy Magee of West Bromwich Albion.

17 The blue and white striped Huddersfield Town jersey with lace-up collar, worn by Roy Goodall in the 1930 FA Cup final.

hipbone, as in charging it will cause considerable pain both to the wearer and his victim.'

In 1904 the FA passed a rule that the knickerbockers worn by players should be long enough to cover the knees. This rule was introduced because it had become the practice of many players to wear, in comparative terms, abbreviated knickerbockers, which the authorities believed was to the discredit of the game's image. Several clubs were in fact fined for being in breach of the rule, but it was relaxed the following year, knickerbockers being required only to reach the knees, and then completely abandoned from the laws of the game in 1907–08.

Shortly afterwards, in 1913, another rule stipulated for the first time that the goalkeeper's jersey must be of a colour distinct from that of the outfield players, and in 1921 an International Board ruling stipulated that in international matches both goalkeepers should wear the same colour – deep yellow or amber. The goalkeeping jersey was usually made of thick knitted wool with a polo-neck collar, and in Football League matches the jersey had to conform to four colours: green, scarlet, blue or white. The goalkeeping jersey still has to be distinct on the field of play, but in recent times the colour stipulations have disappeared.

Another colour ruling occurred in 1924, which saw the introduction of the change strip or 'away' jersey. For the first time, visiting teams were required to change the colour of their strip if their usual colours would clash with those of the home side.

Over the following years, clothing tended to become less and less weighty, although the main force for change lay overseas. Players from the Continent and from South America began wearing close fitting jerseys and what could genuinely be called football shorts and socks, believing this type of outfit would significantly facilitate greater mobility and speed. Although these changes of style were not unnoticed in Britain, there were many reservations as to their suitability for the rigours of a British winter. So either side of the Second World War, British players continued to wear long shorts with plenty of legroom and loose fitting shirts.

It is somewhat surprising to learn that the innovation of shirt numbering was a matter of continued controversy. Even Tottenham Hotspur's proposal of 1933, which asked mildly that 'clubs may number players', was rejected out of hand. The earliest known example of shirt

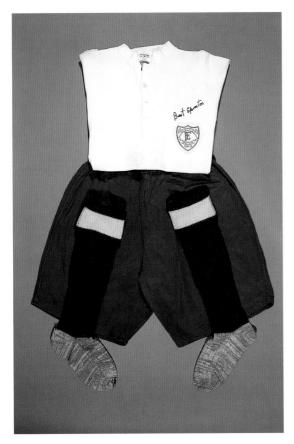

18 Shirt, knickerbockers and stockings worn by Bert Sproston of Manchester City in the Football League v. Scottish League representative match, 1938–39.

19 Northern Ireland and Scotland international shirts, 1950s.

numbering in a senior match occurred on 25 August 1928 when both Chelsea and Arsenal did so in their respective matches. The first official numbering was at the 1933 Cup final, when Everton wore 1–11 and Manchester City 12–22. However, it was not until the abortive 1939–40 season that shirt numbering became compulsory, with the idea prevailing by the narrow margin of 24 votes to 20. As well as helping spectators to identify players easily, especially as stadiums became larger and vantage points more remote, the numbering system proved of great help to reporters and broadcasters, whose duties relied so essentially on accurate factual information. There were many instances of the names of goalscorers, for example, being amended from those originally recorded in the match day accounts.

After the Second World War, the influence of the Continental style player's dress finally broke through the strongly held British traditions. It is

20 The red Wales v. England international shirt worn by Trevor Ford of Sunderland, 1950–51; the white England 'B' v. Luxembourg international shirt worn by Willie Watson of Sunderland, 1950; and the green League of Ireland v. the Football League jersey worn by L. Tuohy of Shamrock Rovers, 1965.

21 The arrival of the designer soccer kit. England jerseys manufactured by Admiral: Kevin Keegan's red, blue and white trimmed England 1982 World Cup Airtex second-choice international jersey; and a Peter Shilton blue-patterned England v. Australia international goalkeeping jersey, 1983.

22 The era of commercial sponsorship:
A red Ian Rush Liverpool jersey; and a blue Gianluca Vialli Chelsea jersey, 1990s.

perhaps not surprising to learn that the man most responsible for this forward-thinking attitude was Sir Matt Busby, Manchester United's legendary manager. Busby began looking to Europe in all footballing respects, entering the first English team in the European Cup of 1956, as well as introducing the first Continental style short-sleeved fitted jersey with a v-neck collar and lightweight shorts for his players at Old Trafford. He was also responsible for the introduction of the first crew- or round-collar jersey, the style that became predominant from the 1960s onwards.

It is difficult to overstate the significance of Hungary's historic defeat of England at Wembley in 1953. The bewildering nature of the Hungarian play, the likes of which the England team had never encountered before, seemed to be further emphasised by the disparity of the teams' attire. The English side, in their impeccably laundered flannel shirts, long shorts and thick woollen stockings, appeared to be from a different age compared to the Hungarian team, in their closely fitted jerseys, abbreviated shorts, and lightweight socks and boots (a subject to be examined shortly) that captain Billy Wright had dismissed as 'ballet shoes' before the game.

After the 1954 World Cup the England kit came under review, and the first step of modernisation was the abandonment of the shirt in favour of the close-fitted jersey with the Continental-style v-neck collar. In the following years, shorts became shorter and many players came to adopt the Continental-style boot.

The 1950s were also a time when major British sportswear manufacturers such as Umbro and Bukta really came into their own, and began supplying their products to many of the country's major clubs at the expense of the traditional local supplier. During the following decade, these fast growing companies took full advantage of the technological advances in methods of manufacture and of synthetic materials such as nylons as the soccer kit revolution continued.

They also met with increasing competition from new sportswear manufacturers, all vying for market share in the global soccer market. Companies such as Admiral, and Adidas, Puma, Hummel and Nike from overseas, became increasingly influential, and the effects of this corporate battling transferred to the designs of the jerseys themselves. Manufacturers began to incorporate their names and logos into the designs of the shirt in an increasingly conspicuous manner. The age of the designer kit had arrived.

At one time the Football Association laid down strict rules governing the colours and patterns on soccer strips. But the rules were then relaxed and further technological advances enabled manufacturers to experiment with multi-coloured and multi-patterned designs on jerseys. Some extreme examples followed, especially on away and goalkeeping jerseys, which did not meet with universal approval, and some strips in particular were derided by horrified fans leading to the toning down of designs and the appeasing of traditionalists by a number of retrospective style jerseys, incorporating features from a bygone era, such as lace-up collars.

In 1979 Scotland became the first international team to have player lettering on the reverse of shirts, and this feature became increasingly popular in the ensuing years for international tournaments based on squad numbers, and in the FA Premier League which also adopted a squad numbering system at the beginning of each season.

The matter of players' boots and boot-studs has always been administered far more closely than other aspects of dress in the laws of the game, because of the inherent dangers of causing injuries to opponents. Originally, any kind of projection on the sole or heels of football boots was strictly banned, the FA laws of 1863 prohibiting spikes, projecting nails and metal plates. Players could be dismissed from the field of play if found to be

infringing the law. In 1891 the laws were relaxed to allow both studs and bars, so long as they were made of leather and did not project more than half an inch. The fastenings had to be driven in flush with the leather, and studs had to be round, not conical or pointed, and not less than half an inch in diameter.

In the nineteenth century it was common for footballers to nail studs into their ordinary ankle-length working boots before the specially designed light-weight football boot began to be used with greater frequency. This was achieved with stud-making kits by which, using a hand stamp, three circles were removed from a strip of leather and nailed together to form a stud.

In *The Book of Football*, a serialised magazine published in twelve fortnightly instalments in season 1905–06, there were fascinating contributions from the famous sports goods-maker William Shillcock, at a time when sportswear manufacturing had genuinely become an industry. Shillcock revealed that he never allowed his stock room to contain less than £2,000 worth of boots in any given week. The most successful firms were those who possessed the most up-to-date machinery and employed the finest operators as well as workmen for a variety of the hand-finishing elements. By this time firms were using a multitude of different machines and presses for the cutting, shaping and riveting of the leather elements of the boot and for the stud making. Footwear was extremely well made, as one of Shillcock's customers attested. John William Robinson, acclaimed as one of the greatest goalkeepers at the turn of the century, confirmed that he wore a pair of Shillcock boots for practice and over 400 matches during eight successive seasons, and asserted: 'They look like lasting for many years to come'.

The Complete Association Footballer's 1912 recommendations on football

24 Examples of Tom Finney 'player-endorsed' 1950s football boots from the collection of the Football Museum, Preston. Note the changing fashion for a lighter boot with a lower cut.

boots were: 'Never take the field wearing a new pair of boots for the first time, as they always feel somewhat stiff, and one walks or runs as if on stilts. Buy your new boots before you actually need them, have the studs removed, and wear them as ordinary walking boots for some time till the stiffness wears off and they become comfortable. One of the authors gets his boots on the small side and goes wading in them for a week or so: by that time they get wet through, the leather stretches, and the boots soon fit like a glove. He then considers them fit for football.'

As well as ankle-length boots, footballers also wore shin-guards, which were strapped on the outside of the stocking in the manner of abbreviated cricket pads, as opposed to the slim shin-pads of the modern age slipped inside the sock. Their invention has been traditionally attributed to the player Sam Widdowson of Nottingham in 1874, and first introduced in season 1880–81. Ankle-guards were also experimented with, but generally found to impede mobility and neat footwork. A primary reason for this solid type of protection was the 'dreadnought' metal toe-cap, a common manufacturer's feature on early football boots and believed to assist power in kicking the ball. They were no doubt also very effective on the opponent as well! The *Association Footballer* discouraged shin-guards, reassuring readers that 'the pain from a kick is only momentary, and rather apt to wake one up than otherwise. A certain professional said he never played his best until he had his shins kicked. Besides, if one starts early enough, one gets used to it; the shins get harder and harder, until the extra protection makes no difference.' The metal toe-cap was finally outlawed in 1921.

After the Second World War, an increasing number of experiments were conducted with materials, size and shape to discover the best type of boot studs or bars for differing ground conditions. The traditional studs of layered leather were never entirely satisfactory as they tended to wear away unevenly or buckle under stress, and there was always the danger of the nail heads becoming exposed. As a result of these new advances, the laws of the game were revised during the 1950s. Players were now allowed to wear slightly longer studs, and the rules governing shapes were also relaxed. The law now permitted studs made from leather, soft rubber, aluminium, and the new moulded plastic and screw-in types.

There was one possibility that the lawmakers had not thought of as they scrutinised the development of football boots. There was no actual rule to say that a player must wear some form of footwear. FIFA (Fedération Internationale de Football Association) were forced to rush through a rule in this respect before the 1950 World Cup in Brazil. India had qualified through the Asian preliminary competitions, and were a team who played barefooted, the feet and toes simply dressed with plasters and bandages. India refused to accept FIFA's ruling and officially withdrew from the final stages of the competition.

The style of boot was revolutionised in Britain in the 1950s as players favoured the Continental-style boot, designed more like a shoe with the leather uppers cut beneath the ankle. Quality of leather and manufacturing techniques improved rapidly when they fell under the influence and investment of the major sportswear companies, and modern examples look like mere slippers when compared with the boots of yesteryear. Today's typical professional soccer boots are made of kangaroo leather, with moulded plastic soles and aluminium screw-in studs, the latter selected from a variety available and dependent on the prevailing ground conditions.

The modern football also looks very different from the leather-cased bladders of earlier times. It is a myth, however, that they are much lighter. In a dry state, in fact, they weigh only about an ounce less than traditional footballs. The biggest difference is that the outer plastic coating is very efficient in preventing water penetration, a problem that blighted the old leather footballs and made them incredibly heavy in wet and muddy ground conditions.

In the game's prehistory the balls used for 'mob-football' style activities were sometime huge, oversize examples, and there was a good deal of variation in sizes. Many early balls were made of hand-stitched leather and stuffed with horsehair. They could be stitched in four sections, with two vertical and horizontal seams, and later took on a segmented appearance, similar to an orange fruit. Stuffing was replaced by an internal, inflated bladder, and the art of ball making became increasingly efficient, with many differing panelled designs coming into existence.

Returning to Shillcock's contributions in the Edwardian serial publication *The Book of Football*, although he is careful not to give away too many trade secrets, especially in the critical area of leather stretching, he confirms that his footballs were made entirely by hand, including the leather cutting, stitching and lacing. The hard, waterproof leather selected was known as 'cowhide', and was favoured for its combined qualities of durability and pliancy. The firm made upwards of thirty different patterns, ranging from the old-fashioned 'button end' to the 'McGregor', which was evidently the favoured design of this period, and used in many internationals and English Cup finals. Including export orders, Shillcock claimed to be selling between 40,000 and 50,000 footballs every year, and is once said to have received a single order for 6,000 balls.

The original FA Cup trophy, known as the 'Little Tin Idol', was incidentally stolen from Shillcock's Birmingham premises, where it was on public exhibition after Aston Villa had won it in 1895. It was never recovered.

The Football Association in 1883 specified a regulation size of football. Law 2 adopted the specification of the FA Cup rules, and this was further clarified in 1889. The rule stated: 'The Circumference of the association ball shall be not less than 27 inches and not more than 28 inches. In International matches, at the commencement of the game, the weight of the ball shall be from 12 to 15 ounces.' In 1937 the parameters of the weight of the ball were increased to 14 to 16 ounces, and the phrase 'international matches' was later deleted from the rules, making the size and weight of the ball regulation for all senior matches.

In 1905 an addition to the law was made: 'The outer casing of the ball must be of leather, and no materials shall be used in construction of the ball that would constitute a danger to the players.' This was a response to experiments with the use of rubber balls and other innovations, which alleviated the problems connected with leather balls in wet conditions, but proved highly unsatisfactory to play with.

The notorious laces used in football manufacturing could be extremely unpleasant when making direct contact with the player while heading, and especially dangerous around the eye. An alternative to the laced football bladder was the leather ball with a pneumatic valve. To be prepared for the match, the ball simply needed to be inflated by an air pump inserted into the external valve of the bladder. It was some time, however, before manufacturing techniques were improved, and punctures were common. Repair was also expensive; the ball had to be returned to the manufacturer for there was no opening to remove the bladder as there was with the laced ball. A later halfway-house solution was the introduction of the pre-laced valve ball. The advantage of this type was that the ball could be inflated and deflated without interfering with the lacing, and if the ball was to puncture, the bladder could be removed by undoing the lacing and repaired on the spot.

25 A selection of leather footballs dating between the late nineteenth century and the 1950s, comprising a large Kirkwall-style ball, early segmented footballs, and twelve, eighteen and T-panel balls.

Puncturing was a particular problem immediately after the Second World War, owing to the unavailability of high-quality leather. In the first two postwar Wembley FA Cup finals of 1946 and 1947, the ball burst on both occasions.

The introduction of floodlit matches led to further experiment, as the traditional dark brown leather ball was far from satisfactory in artificial light. Similar troubles had always arisen on dark days as well. Coatings of various kinds were tried in white and light yellow, and later a ball of orange coloured leather was produced, and immortalised by its use in the 1966 World Cup final. The ball that burst in the 1947 FA Cup final was of the light yellow type, while the white ball had in fact been experimented with by Herbert Chapman, Arsenal's innovative manager, as early as the 1930s. The white ball was not introduced officially, however, until 1951 and traditions dictated that the brown ball was still to dominate for the next twenty years or so. Referees were later given powers to change the ball for one of a lighter colour if necessary during the course of a match. Eventually manufacturing techniques were perfected and enabled the plastic covered ball to solve the age-old problem of sodden leather, and this type of ball quickly became the norm, much to the good of the game.

chapter four

Commemorative and Decorative Objects

The commemoration of events and characters in a variety of forms is a long and peculiarly British tradition. Kings and queens, politicians, battles, sporting events and other subjects have all been recorded for posterity. The purpose of the commemorative items was to give some permanence to events or individuals that held the nation's attention at a particular moment. In soccer this extends to great teams and their triumphs, significant occasions and outstanding individuals.

There is a particularly strong tradition in ceramics. The earliest event to be commemorated in this fashion was the coronation of King Charles II in 1660. Such items, however, were exceptional pieces and the manufacture of commemorative pottery was rare until the reign of George III. From about 1780 onwards such production steadily increased, reaching its crescendo with Queen Victoria's Diamond Jubilee in 1897.

It was the advent of mass production techniques, however, that accelerated the commercial possibilities for manufacturers, and opened up new markets such as that for soccer, which required basic and inexpensive products to reach its potential audience. This was helped by the development of new ceramics such as creamware, invented by Josiah Wedgwood, which could be produced quickly and economically and was far easier to decorate. But, it was the invention of transfer printing to earthenware that was the key breakthrough. It was said that the output of one man transfer-printing wares was equal to that of fifty decorators painting by hand, and the process became the commonest method of decoration in use.

The depiction of soccer, and sport in general, in commemorative wares is comparatively slight. Anonymous Staffordshire factories began producing a number of earthenware mugs and other vessels from around the 1860s onwards, transfer-printed with general soccer themes, but true commemoratives are scarce before the 1890s. Sheffield Wednedsay FC are well represented in commemoratives, with examples illustrated here from all three of their FA Cup final victories between 1896 and 1935. They would also appear to have been one of the earliest clubs to be associated with such wares. An earthenware mug (26, bottom left) was made to commemorate the Yorkshire club's success in the 1896 FA Cup.

A finer example was the blue transfer-printed plate (27) made by the

26 A selection of commemorative and decorative ceramics.

43

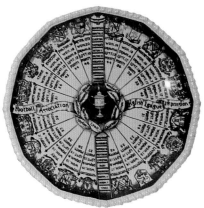

Bristol Porcelain & Glass company to commemorate the 1906–07 season. Again Sheffield Wednesday are featured, at this was their second Cup-winning season, together with Newcastle United who won the League Championship. This would have been a more expensive item manufactured in porcelain, with its complex printing which incorporates a central portrayal of the FA Cup trophy, club crests and details of their playing records for the season. It was probably beyond the financial reach of many fans and appears not to have been a great success for the manufacturers. Although this example surfaces fairly regularly, it was almost certainly a one off, since no other similar plates are known to exist for other seasons.

By 1935, the year of Wednesday's third FA Cup victory, the club commemorative was a more affordable porcelain mug (26, centre-left) made by the Bell China Company, with simple printed details of the team's road to Wembley.

Royalty has been a far more popular subject for commemorative ceramics, and in 1937 an opportunity arose to combine this theme with soccer and to attract wider public interest. To commemorate the Coronation Cup Final between Sunderland and Preston North End, the Royal Ivory factory produced a plate (26, bottom-right) with a central polychrome print of King George VI and Queen Elizabeth above the match inscription, within in a blue feathered border.

The theme of commemorative soccer wares continued after the war, where it often fell into the remit of the limited edition souvenir marking clubs' outstanding achievements and also focusing on specific stars. Bobby Charlton, for example, became the subject of a commemorative plate produced in 1970 by the Crown Staffordshire factory in recognition of the Manchester United player gaining his hundredth international cap. A similar item (28) was produced to commemorate Peter Shilton's all-time England record of 125 caps, won between 1970 and 1990. It is decorated with a central portrait of the player, with the border printed with a blue England cap and details of all the nations he played against to set the record.

Many of the decorative ceramics on soccer themes produced over the years follow the pattern of commemorative wares and are usually basic, inexpensive items. These include a number of decorative pieces made of earthenware from the Staffordshire factories, with colourful polychrome prints of match action. These designs appeared on a variety of household pieces including beakers (26, top left), cups and saucers, milk jugs, sugar bowls, and tankards and so on. Similar items were produced on the Continent and are typically fancier articles, such as the illustrated chocolate cup (26, centre-right) which has a coloured soccer print in the centre, similar to the Staffordshire beaker, but it is made to a delicate design and highly gilded in Continental taste.

27 Bristol Porcelain & Glass Company plate commemorating the 1906–07 season.

28 Limited edition porcelain plate commemorating Peter Shilton's 125 England caps.

29 St Armand plate, French, 1920s.

30 Longwy enamelled plate, French, 1950s.

Children's wares also proved popular, a child's bed-warming plate, for example (26 top centre), mounted in a metal hot-water vessel and decorated with teddy bears playing soccer and other sports.

Other popular items include the miniature armorial and crested wares made by firms such as Goss, Carlton and Grays. These were inexpensive to produce and the same item could be targeted at regional markets by the inclusion of different town and city arms, or by decorating footballers in the local team colours. Examples here illustrated include a Grays miniature moonflask (26, top right) from their Sports China series, made c.1910, and decorated with a footballer in the red and white stripes of Exeter City, then a Southern League side. The small ashtray at the centre of the illustration is from the Carlton Ware British Sports Series in the early part of the century, and is themed to Barnsley FC. The ashtray is decorated with a polychrome transfer print of Round Tower, Edge Hill, and inscribed 'Play Up Barnsley'.

The Art Deco period is noted for its novelty wares. In soccer these included such wares as a teapot (26, bottom centre) made by Sadler's of Burslem which remained popular for a number of years and can be found decorated in many team colours. The body simulates a brown leather-

panelled football, while a player taking a throw in, this example decorated in claret and blue hoops, forms the handle. The spout is designed as a silver referee's whistle, and the knop of the cover is modelled as the FA Cup trophy.

French factories liked to inject some humour into their soccer wares. During the 1920s the St Armand factory produced a number of cartoon-style wares, which typically depicted humorous or slapstick match incidents, such as a goalkeeper being hit full in the face by a forward's shot (26, centre left), or another goalkeeper distracted from his duties by a beauty applying her lipstick (29).

A very colourful French plate is the example produced by Longwy for St. Etienne FC in the 1950s (30). Longwy Co. was formed over 200 years ago and is famous for the crackle glazes it developed as a result of using wood-burning fires which gave an uneven temperature during production, causing the desired 'fault' in the glaze. The border is beautifully enamelled with a colourful repeated design interspersed by panelled footballs, while the centre of the plate is hand painted with a footballing scene. It is the work of two decorators, Paul Mignon (enameller) and Albert Kirchterre (painter).

Spelter is the most common medium found in decorative metalware depicting soccer. It is made from zinc and was first introduced as a technical innovation at the Great Exhibition of 1851, where it aroused considerable interest. The production costs in casting spelter were far less than when using bronze, and the material could be made to mimic the appearance of the more expensive metal, produced with tints of colour or decorated by painting. It was therefore an appropriate and adaptable material for use in the soccer market. The drawback is that spelter is a far less durable metal than bronze, and is particularly susceptible to damage and wear.

31 A French spelter figure commemorating the goalkeeper Alex Thépot.

There were, however, a good number of bronze footballing groups cast, especially during the amateur era up to the time of the Great War, when potential patrons for high-quality works were in greater abundance.

The technical aspects of bronze-making had been revolutionised during the nineteenth century, especially by the great foundries of France which enjoyed a golden period in this era. The traditional method was known as the cire perdue (lost wax) process, in which a mould was formed over a wax model of the subject, which melted out with the introduction of molten bronze. This method was increasingly abandoned in favour of sand casting where the original model could be preserved after the mould had been formed around it, thereby allowing the cast to be replicated for further editions. The only disadvantage was that the mould had to be chiselled away from the surface of the cast, with any roughness smoothed out. In this respect the skills of the bronze founder were nearly as important as those of

32 Edouard Drouot
(French, 1859–1945)
A footballer about to strike the
ball (one of a pair)
Bronze, c.1900.

33 H. Fugère (French)
A running footballler
Spelter, c.1900.

the sculptor, for the same reasons that a poor print engraver could ruin the original design of the artist. This new technique accelerated public interest in what were now more affordable, quality bronzes.

Sadly, many soccer bronzes are unsigned by the sculptor and bear no foundry marks, which makes research of these largely anonymous items very difficult. It is particularly rewarding, therefore, when signed pieces make an appearance, such as examples of the work of the French sculptor Edouard Drouot (1859–1945).

The finely sculpted Drouot footballer (32) was one of a pair, its companion figure portraying a rugby footballer. They were exhibited at the Exposition Universelle in Paris in 1900, the year in which the French capital hosted the second Olympic Games.

Compare Drouot's bronze figure to the spelter figure of the running footballer by the French sculptor H. Fugère, which dates from the same period (33). The finishing of the spelter example is visibly inferior, and lacks the detail so evident in the bronze casting, such as the creases in the player's shirt and shorts, the muscles delineated in his limbs, and even the lacing on

34 A group of decorative metalware.

35 A pair of original Victorian cast-iron turnstiles from Anfield, Liverpool FC.

the panelled football. It also lacks the deep, rich patination that could be achieved in bronze.

An example of commemorative metalware is the anonymous French spelter figure cast in honour of Alex Thépot, the celebrated French goalkeeper who played thirty-one times for France between 1927 and 1935, including the first two World Cups of 1930 and 1934 (31). He was regarded as one of the greatest goalkeepers in the world, and this particular figure was made specifically in recognition of his bravery in the match against Mexico in Montevideo on 13 July 1930, the very first match in World Cup finals history. Thé Pot suffered an horrific injury when he was kicked in the jaw after only ten minutes of the match and had to go off. Two days later he took the field again in the match against Argentina, producing an outstanding performance and denying the opposition on many occasions before he was finally unsighted and beaten in the eighty-first minute. At the end of the game he was carried from the field of play by delighted supporters.

The group illustration (34) shows a variety of soccer figures cast mostly in spelter and bronze, including a large signed spelter group by the French sculptor Emile Picault (1839–1915). However, the finely modelled group with a silvery appearance, modelled as two footballers challenging for possession of the ball, is made from a different material known as Kayserzinn. The metal, which is a kind of art pewter, takes its name from the German company of J. P. Kayser & Söhne (1885–c.1904), whose foundry was situated at Krefeld-Bochum near Düsseldorf. They employed pioneering methods in the production of pewter which did not resort to electroplating, as did the famous WMF (Württembergische Metallwarenfabrik) with their pewter. High standards of casting were achieved using a strong malleable alloy of tin, copper and antimony, which gave the fine silvery shine after polishing. Kayserzinn became the inspiration for the famous Liberty Tudric range of pewterware.

A larger scale form of decorative metalware comes from the field of architectural salvage. Two of the original red painted cast-iron Victorian turnstiles installed at the Anfield Road End of the ground of Liverpool FC (35) were salvaged when this part of the stadium was redeveloped at the end of the 1996–97 season, thereby preserving these important items of soccer heritage. They are fine examples of Victorian workmanship and were manufactured by the engineering firm of W. T. Ellison & Co. Ltd of Salford, Manchester, and

49

patented as the 'Ellison's rush preventative turnstile'. They were designed in semi-circular form with moulded tops, above tubular supports decorated with pierced trellis panels. The revolving action of the turnstile navigates four gates, controlled by a brake pedal.

Another highly decorative item, remarkable for its size and its unusual nature, is a pub mirror (36) manufactured by F. O'Neil & Son of Glasgow in the late nineteenth century. The mirror plate, measuring 106 by 244 cm (96 in), is centred by a fine reverse-painted panel, depicting a soccer match, within a gilt border punctuated by anthemia, and contained in a moulded and painted frame. The painting captures the spirit of the sport at this period quite beautifully, and the artist has seemingly achieved the feat of making time stand still.

In addition to these grander works, soccer has found its way onto a great variety of everyday utilitarian objects, usually gentlemen's accessories of one description or another. The ball has proved to be a popular design inspiration for smoking accessories including vestas (37), desk equipment including an inkwell (38), and a 1960s ice bucket (39), the last being a variation of the famous kitsch pineapple ice bucket, the popular drinks accessory of the period.

A tradition with its roots in the Victorian period is the decorative tin, especially the biscuit tin – an example of art in commerce and marketing, and a field keenly collected today. In fact, these tins were always designed to be kept, for as well as providing decorative packaging, they could be reused in the home as containers for items other than the original biscuits.

The biscuit manufacturers who commissioned these tins realised that not

36 A large reverse-painted Victorian pub mirror.

37 A silvered metal vesta.

38 A metal-mounted stoneware inkwell.

39 1960s plastic ice bucket.

40 An aluminium Huntley & Palmers biscuit tin in the form of the FA Cup trophy.

only was it necessary to have a superior design, but also designs that would tap the broadest possible public interest. Multitudes of themes, shapes and printed decoration were therefore introduced over the years, including examples depicting popular sports including soccer.

The aluminium tin in the form of the FA Cup Trophy (40) is most interesting and very rare. It was commissioned by the famous Reading biscuit firm of Huntley & Palmers in 1927, and probably manufactured by N. C. Joseph Ltd of Stratford-on-Avon, who were pioneers in Great Britain in making aluminium containers. Reading FC, who were sometimes known as the 'Biscuit Men', had reached the semi-final of the FA Cup in

41 After Isaac Robert Cruikshank (1786–1856) Foot Ball. Coloured aquatint by George Hunt.

42 After Thomas Webster RA (1800–86) The Foot-Ball. Coloured print.

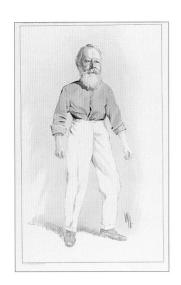

43 Portrait of Lord Kinnaird, First President of the Football Association. Vanity Fair coloured lithograph, signed: W.H.

44 Famous English Football Players, 1881. A team-group caprice of leading players from the first decade of the FA Cup: coloured lithograph published with the *Boy's Own Paper*. Standing (left to right): Charles Campbell, Charles Caborn, Tom Marshall, Harry Sweepstone, John Hunter, Sam Widdowson, Edwin Luntley, James Prinsep, Harry McNeil, William Lindsay, John Sands, Tom Brindle, William Mosforth; seated (left to right) Herbert Whitfield, Norman Bailey, Edward Bambridge, Francis Sparks and F. W. Earp.

1927, the finest cup run in their entire history. Huntley & Palmers then commissioned the tin in anticipation of the club reaching the Wembley final, believing the biscuit tin would becoming a lucrative local souvenir. Unfortunately, Cardiff City spoiled the party in the semi-final and the biscuit firm withdrew the idea. The overwhelming majority of the tins were re-routed for the export market and are therefore very hard to find. The illustrated example is remarkable in that it is still complete with its original favour, inscribed with 'The Road to Wembley' and a badge in the form of Huntley & Palmers' famous Osborne biscuit. It is a brilliant marketing item, the reverse of the Osborne biscuit forming a lady's vanity mirror, which would have made the souvenir equally attractive to all members of the household.

In comparison with many other sports, the subject of soccer has been poorly served by the arts over the years, although this is more likely to have been through a lack of patronage than artists' reluctance to be inspired by the sport. In 1953, in celebration of their ninetieth anniversary, the Football Association attempted to encourage artists by organising a soccer exhibition at Park Lane House, London. The FA received 1,700 submissions of which 150 were selected and shown.

With many historical soccer paintings now in private or institutional collections, there is a paucity of original works available to collectors. Some early paintings from the nineteenth century, however, were engraved as prints.

Isaac Robert Cruickshank drew barrack square soccer scenes, from which aquatints were published by George and Charles Hunt of Covent Garden in 1820 and 1827. Cruickshank's lively and amusing works depict rough-and-tumble military soccer matches contested by men of all ranks (41).

In 1839 Thomas Webster RA, a confirmed sporting enthusiast, exhibited his 'Football Match' with success at the Royal Academy. The picture was

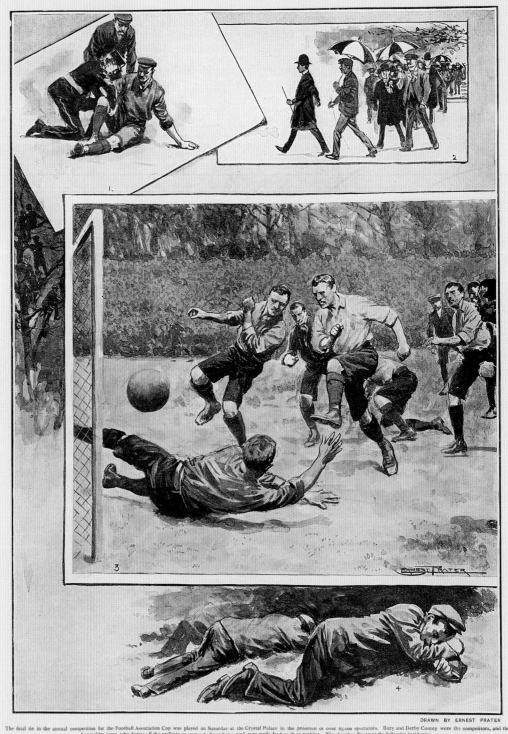

DRAWN BY ERNEST PRATER

The final tie in the annual competition for the Football Association Cup was played on Saturday at the Crystal Palace in the presence of over 63,000 spectators. Bury and Derby County were the competitors, and the Lancashire team, who during all the preliminary games had not lost a goal, won easily by 6 goals to nothing. The sketches illustrate the following incidents :—

No. 1—Attending to the injured goalkeeper   No. 2—Wearing the colours and carrying umbrellas of rival teams
No. 3—Bury scoring   No. 4—Travellers from the north who slept through the match

subsequently copied by other artists and also engraved. The coloured print (42) after Webster was published in Germany in the second half of the nineteenth century.

As the sport grew in popularity around the turn of the century, it was featured more regularly by the popular magazines and periodicals of the day and by their illustrators. The famous *Vanity Fair* magazine ran a series titled 'Men of the Day', which included a coloured supplement print of Lord Kinnaird (43), the first President of the Football Association; while *Boys' Own Magazine* produced a delightful image of famous English football players of 1881 (44). The group actually contains two Scottish players, Charles Campbell and Harry McNeil of Queen's Park and Scotland; they were, however, familiar figures in the English game through the Glasgow club's participation in the FA Cup in the 1870s and 1880s.

45 After Ernest Prater (fl.1897–1914) The Final Tie for the Football Association Cup, Derby County and Bury at the Crystal Palace: coloured print with four vignettes and an accompanying key.

46 Amos Ramsbottom (1889–1967). Woolwich Arsenal win at Blackburn, 1906.

55

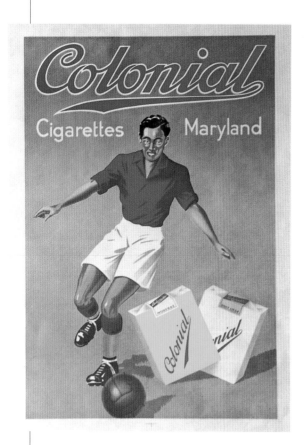

47 (opposite) Valencia FC v.
Seleccion de la Escuadra
Inglesa, 15 April 1929. Spanish
colour lithographic promotional
match poster, signed Forno, for
a Valencia match against an
English XI.

48 Colonial Cigarettes,
Maryland: an American colour
lithographic advertisement
poster, c.1940.

49 Fussball – Weltmeisterschaft,
Chile, 1962: German colour lithographic advertisement poster
promoting a film of the 1962
World Cup.

50 Donat Gauri;
An aerial duel.
A Spanish colour lithographic
poster, 1963.

URUGUAY
TURISMO 1942

XIV CAMPEONATO
SUDAMERICANO
de FOOTBALL

51 (previous page) The official poster for the South American football championship, 1942, colour lithograph.

52 Johan Otto von Sprechelsen Liberte pour les footballeurs – Le Président Cantona la Nouvelle République! A colour lithographic poster portraying Eric Cantona and promoting 'Nikepark', France, 8 June to 12 July 1998.

53 Guillermo Laborde (1886–1940). The official poster of the 1930 World Cup, colour lithograph.

An illustrator who was particularly attracted to football was Ernest Prater (fl.1897–1914), who contributed to a number of magazines including *The Black and White, The Sphere, The Graphic* and *The Boys' Own Paper*. An example of a print after his work (45) includes vignettes of the FA Cup Final between Derby County and Bury, played at the Crystal Palace in 1903. Amos Ramsbottom (46) was an artist who captured the goals and incidents from games for illustrating match reports in newspapers. A mark of his quality was that he took the trouble to colour his drawings, even though they would be reproduced in black and white in the papers.

As well as prints, an array of posters have been published over the years. The illustrated examples (47–53) are from the Continent and were produced for promotional purposes, including the advertising of football matches, cigarettes and films. During the 1998 World Cup in France, Eric Cantona became the central subject of a poster (52) promoting Nikepark, an event organised by the famous sportswear manufacturer, Nike; its unusual and stylish design is intended to be in the manner of a political poster from the former communist bloc. The tradition of World Cup posters was set in place at the inaugural tournament held in Uruguay (53) in 1930.

Cumming. "Manchester City's Forward Line." Browell. Cartwright.
Taylor. Howard.

MANCHESTER UNITED FOOTBALL CLUB, 1914-15.

Back row : J. McGough (Asst. Trainer), J. W. Mew, Jas. Hodge, W. Wright, L. Moores, A. Allman, E. K. Hudson (Linesman)
Second row : H. Dale (Referee), W. Meredith, T. Capps, G. Wall, T. Ashworth, G. Anderson, S. Cubberley, r. O. Connor
G. Stacey, R. Davies (Trainer).
Front row : Mr. J. Taylor, J. Norton, G. E. Travers, E. J. West, t. Hunter, A. Potts, A. Woodcock, W. H. Eaves, F. Knowles
Photo, Chambers, Croydon.

J. Cantwell. A. Grimsdell. B. Bliss.
Official Photo 1920

BEFORE THE MATCH

BIRTHDAY WISHES.

I know that you'll be lucky,
I hope you're happy too.
Each hour from morn till bedtime
Bring some new joy for you.

THE WINNER.

A player looking very smart,
She wins the game and wins the heart.

"That reminds me – I must blow out my football when I get home!"

A HARD WORKER

FOOTBALL INCIDENTS.
Oxford & Cambridge Association.

chapter five

Miscellaneous Ephemera and Collectables

A very popular category of collecting is the area of soccer cards (54–58). This can be broken down into the broad sub-categories of postcards, cigarette cards and trade cards, of which the latter is the broadest.

The so-called 'Golden Age' of postcards spans the Edwardian and immediate pre-First World War era. In 1894 the Post Office had allowed postcards to be used with a separately affixed postage stamp, and this decision opened the way for private companies to produce their own pictorial cards. This potential was aided further in 1899 by the relaxation of rules regarding size restrictions, and the larger, standard sized card was born. A multitude of themes appeared on postcards, and postcard mania swept through the land, with the popularity of the inexpensive, decorative card not subsiding until after the Great War. This period coincided with the spiralling interest in soccer, and not surprisingly the sport proved a successful theme for the pictorial postcard, featuring the famous players and teams of the day, which were often published in numbered series.

The earliest cards were produced by printing processes known as gravure, collotype and half-tone, and have a matt appearance, but they were quickly joined by examples manufactured by photographic processes, known as 'real photographic', or more commonly 'real photo' cards, which possessed a glossy finish.

As well as formal-style cards of team groups and personalities, a number of humorous and whimsical postcards began to emerge that are very typical of the Edwardian era, and characteristic of the entire British postcard art-form, epitomised by the work of Donald McGill. Colour, too, became an increasing feature, and this allowed publishers to move into various artist-drawn areas such as team colours and action pictures; match action could also be hand-tinted over photographs. The commemoration of major games such as English Cup finals became an increasing feature of the souvenir postcard, and the breadth of other miscellaneous subjects was never to be bettered.

Although in recent years interest has gathered a pace in post-1920 examples, which at one time were rather disregarded by the serious collector, it is certainly true that the quantity and scope of postcards fell away sharply from this date. They became largely the domain of the local photographer

54 A miscellany of soccer postcards.

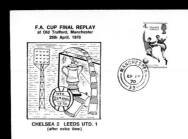

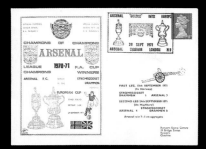

55 A selection of soccer philatelic covers.

56 A set of sixteen first-day cover postcards for the 1958 World Cup in Sweden.

57 (p. 63) A miscellany of soccer cigarette and trade cards.

A. R. FENWICK

COVENTRY CITY

FULHAM F.C.

D. McKINLAY

LIVERPOOL

F.Osborne

PLAYER'S CIGARETTES

ASSOCIATION CUP WINNERS
THE OLD CUP

Photo L'ÉQUIPE. Offert par Biscuits REM - Reims

François MILAZZO

François MILAZZO
(9-2-1934)
Demi ou Inter

Un très beau footballeur,
élégant, bien découplé, grand
(1 m 78) très brun (Milazzo
est né à MEKNES au MAROC).
Ses qualités sont essentielle-
ment la vaillance, la comba-
tivité, l'activité. Mais il possède
également un tir remarquable
qui lui permet de réussir aussi
bien comme inter que comme
demi.

E. SCOTT

LIVERPOOL

PLAYER'S CIGARETTES

ASSOCIATION CUP WINNERS.
NEWCASTLE UNITED. 1924

Photo L'ÉQUIPE. Offert par Biscuits REM - Reims

Dominique COLONNA

Dominique COLONNA
(4-9-1928)
Gardien de but

Offert par la Corse au Football français. Sympathique,
d'une grande simplicité,
"DOUME" est le plus racé
des gardiens de but français
actuels. Souple, rapide, cou-
rageux, il est aussi clairvoyant
et équilibré. A souvent sauvé
REIMS et l'équipe de FRANCE.

PLAYER'S CIGARETTES

ASSOCIATION CUP WINNERS
THE PRESENT CUP

W. DEAN

CHURCHMAN'S CIGARETTES

W. HALL (TOTTENHAM HOTSPUR)

PLAYER'S CIGARETTES

ASSOCIATION CUP WINNERS
THE MEDALS

WEST HAM UNITED F.C.

PARTICK THISTLE F.C.

preparing formal player and team-group portraits. The variety had disappeared, with only a handful of exceptions, and so had the extraordinary interest of the earlier years.

One of the problems facing the postcard in the interwar years was competition in the form of giveaways by the tobacco companies and the famous magazines of the day. A new form of soccer card collecting had begun which, although not entirely extinguishing the postcard tradition, certainly became the greater collecting interest.

First-day covers are an area where the two keen collecting fields of postcards (cartology or deltiology) and postage stamps (philately) merge with a common interest. In Britain the first decorative philatelic covers incorporating soccer subjects were issued in conjunction with the 1966 World Cup. Furthermore, these postage stamps were the first ever examples from Britain featuring sportsmen in action.

Before the tournament, on 1 June, three postage stamps were issued in three denominations – 4d, 6d and 1s 3d. There had been some last-minute changes of design on one example: the original concept displayed the flags of the sixteen competing nations, but political and diplomatic pressure led to its withdrawal as it incorporated the flag of North Korea. The stamps and the philatelic covers, nevertheless, were an immediate success. It is not surprising, therefore, that a second version of the fourpenny postage stamp, overprinted 'England Winners', generated more interest than any other British stamp had ever done when it was issued on 18 August 1966. A strictly limited edition of twelve million copies had been produced, and such was the demand that post offices reported that their supplies were sold out within minutes of opening on the day of issue.

The World Cup Willie postcard in the centre of the illustration (55) bears the first day of issue postmark of 'Harrow and Wembley'; the autograph of the England captain Bobby Moore also enhances its collecting interest. Surrounding the central card in this illustration are other examples of philatelic covers commemorating famous clubs and matches, including a 1970 World Cup example autographed by the England manager Sir Alf Ramsey.

There has been a far older tradition of soccer-themed postage stamps overseas, especially in connection with previous World Cups or in commemoration of soccer tournaments within the Olympic Games. In 1958 the World Cup hosts Sweden produced a special set of sixteen first-day cover decorative colour postcards (56), depicting players in action and topographical views of the towns where the matches were to be played.

Soccer is amongst the oldest established topics for cigarette cards, with the first examples produced by Ogden's Ltd in the 1890s. It is certainly one of the largest topics too, with an estimated 10,000 different footballing cards produced by the tobacco companies in the first half of the century. Consequently, cigarette cards represent a formidable source of valuable pictorial and historical information on the development of the sport and the personalities it has produced.

Cigarette cards gained popularity in the immediate pre-First World War period and came to be issued with greater frequency, typically in sets of twenty five or fifty, but sometimes in massive collections numbering well over 1,000. By the 1930s cigarette-card collecting had become a serious hobby and all the major tobacco companies were producing soccer subjects, including famous firms such as John Player, Wills, Gallaher and Churchman's. Their appearance ranges from black and white and sepia-toned photographic examples to hand-coloured cards including artist-drawn portraits and caricatures.

Special albums were produced for the collector to keep the cards, and the adhesive-backed card was also produced, although this idea is not as desirable to the present-day collector, who prefers loose examples.

The majority of cards feature prominent players and teams, and these sets were revised or supplemented regularly as new stars emerged and others faded away. The cards, however, began to explore other aspects of the game too, and a good deal of informative variety exists. Typical examples of these sets would include English Cup and Championship winners, sporting trophies, soccer terminology and skills, club colours, nicknames and crests,

58 A hand-coloured plate from the Miss Blanche Spelfoto's album, published by the Vittora Egyptian Cigarette Company of Rotterdam.

international caps and badges, club captains, the laws of the game and many others.

Worthy of specific mention are the cards of Godfrey Phillips Ltd, universally known as 'Pinnace' cards, after the specific brand name in which they were presented, although not until this famous series had been in existence for three years. They are unusual in that they were produced in three different sizes – miniature, large and cabinet size. The cabinet cards were only available either with boxes of fifty cigarettes or in exchange for twenty-five miniature cards returned to the manufacturer in reusable condition.

The cigarette companies on the Continent were active in these areas too. The Vittora Egyptian Cigarette Company of Rotterdam published a magnificent cloth-bound album called Miss Blanche Spelfoto's, Competitie Wedstryden. One hundred hand-coloured action photographs by Polygoon were contained with the lavish work, which depict League and International action from Holland in season 1932–33. The present image (58) portrays the Holland v. Belgium encounter in Amsterdam on 7 May 1933. Each photograph is laid down on grey mounts with gilt edging and is accompanied by a printed legend detailing the match.

Other commercial operations soon took account of the appeal of the soccer-themed giveaway, and how they encouraged sales and promoted brand loyalty. The *Topical Times* offered picture cards to its readers in the 1930s, which include real photo style examples and the more impressive hand-coloured photographic portraits (60). The elongated versions were known as 'panel portraits'.

59 Robertson's Golly soccer figures.

Picture cards began to be issued with an array of different products, including other popular magazines, newspapers and periodicals, as well as by food, beverage and confectionery makers. They also began to target the young directly in a way that the cigarette cards could not, through the sales of comics, boys' interest magazines, sweets and bubble gum. Generally speaking, trade cards are of an inferior quality to those of the 'golden age' of cigarette cards.

The same principle of the picture card was applied to other types of give-aways. Customers of Robertson's preserves, for example, could send away for footballing figures (59) modelled as their famous Golly trademark.

An area especially pioneered by the ESSO petroleum company was the series of coin or medal collections given away free with the purchase of petrol. These include the sets themed around the 1970 World Cup and the centenary of the FA Cup in 1972, as well as small soccer-knowledge booklets which were also produced and known as Squelchers.

The popularity of the soccer medal collection made a renaissance during the 1998 World Cup in France. The supermarket Sainsbury's, who were endorsed by the Football Association as the 'Official England Supermarket', offered a wide range of soccer merchandise as World Cup fever swept across the land. The centrepiece of the promotion was their medal collection (61). The medals were struck with the images of Glenn Hoddle and twenty-two players before the England squad was announced. A limited edition set of five medals was therefore produced subsequently, covering the players who had not been anticipated earlier.

60 *Topical Times* portrait and panel cards featuring:

(top, left to right) Jimmy Allen (Aston Villa) and Edward Catlin (Sheffield Wednesday).

(bottom, left to right) Joe Mercer (Everton), Alec Hastings (Sunderland), Jack Crayston (Arsenal) and Bert Sproston (Leeds United).

On other occasions, similar items were not give-aways but the product themselves. The sticker album became a popular collectable in the 1970s, including the *Soccer Stars* (62) and *World Cup Soccer Stars* series published by FKS. Another name to come to prominence in this respect was Panini.

Badge collecting is another highly popular hobby amongst soccer enthusiasts, an area that is ably supported by a collectors' association, the details of which are listed at the back of this book. The largest area of collecting in this category concerns the multitude of supporters' badges that have been produced over many years, and that have long been a popular item in the club souvenir shop. There are other types of badges that were not generally available to the public, such as those issued to stewards and officials on duty at matches, and these are of course much scarcer items. There was also a distinct continental tradition of club-badge swapping by players, much in the same way that players exchange jerseys after matches. Many clubs in Europe produced these badges for their players specifically for this purpose.

61 The Sainsbury's England 1998 World Cup squad medal collection.

62 FKS *Soccer Stars* sticker album, 1970s.

The badges illustrated (63) are the type produced for supporters, and these examples date mainly from the 1970s. They are colourfully enamelled on gilt-metal and typically bear the design of the club's crest. The tradition is a good deal older than this, however, an example being the badge on the Bolton Wanderers favour (64). The favour was the forerunner of the more familiar rosette, with the present example being produced for the occasion of the 1894 FA Cup final played at Goodison Park, Liverpool. From beneath the badge decorated in the team colours and a pair of 'Bowton Trotters', two ribbons are suspended bearing the name of the club. Sadly, the team could not fulfil the urgings of the badge's inscription, with the Wanderers crashing to a 1-4 defeat against Notts County. These items are now very scarce.

Either side of the favour (64) can be seen examples from a different area of badge collecting. On the left is a cloth shirt badge relating to the referee for the Wales v. Belgium international match played at Cardiff on 23 November 1949. This was a memorable day for the Welsh, with the team recording a comprehensive 5-1 victory. The other, finely embroidered in gold wire, is an England blazer badge relating to the so-called Victory international matches of 1945 and 1946. England played a total of five of these games at the end of the wartime

63 Metal and enamel supporters' badges, 1970s.

64 (Left to right):
A shirt badge awarded to Luton referee, Henry Pearce, who officiated at the Wales v. Belgium international match played at Ninian Park, Cardiff, 23 November 1949; a Bolton Wanderers favour for the 1894 FA Cup final; and a blazer badge awarded to all England players who took part in the Victory internationals of 1945–46.

65 An FA illuminated address presented to Jack Crayston of Arsenal for representing England in wartime internationals.

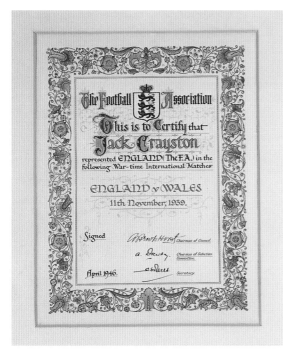

period. They were not classified as official international matches (neither were the earlier wartime internationals), and accordingly caps were not awarded. Players were, however, allowed to keep these decorative badges as souvenirs. At the end of the war, every England player who participated in a wartime international was also presented with a very decorative illuminated address (65) by the Football Association in honour of their achievements. The illustrated example was presented to the Arsenal player Jack Crayston, who played just the one match, the very first wartime international, against Wales at Cardiff on Armistice Day, 1939. Addresses presented to players for several wartime appearances have multiple match inscriptions in the reserved area accordingly.

A long tradition in international soccer, especially popular on the Continent, is the practice of opposing captains exchanging pennants (66) from their respective Football Associations before the commencement of the match. Pennants generate considerable interest on the rare occasions that they become available to the collector.

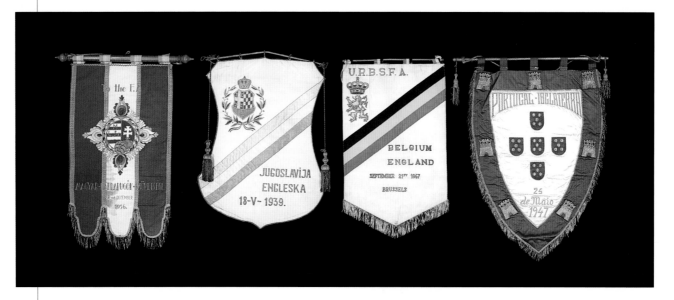

The workmanship on early examples is particularly fine. They are nearly always made of coloured silk, often conforming to the colours of the national flag, with appliqué and embroidered match inscriptions, heraldic symbols and very often the official crest of the national Football Association. Typically, they are further embellished with wirework fringes and tassels and are sometimes found on the original wooden or metal display poles. In later years the size of pennants decreased and they lacked the elaboration of the earlier examples. Their interest is enhanced when they relate to particularly famous or historic matches, such as England's staggering 10-0 victory over Portugal in Lisbon in 1947.

From the 1860s onwards new factory manufacturing methods made children's toys and games more accessible and affordable. Before this date many amusements were simply produced as sidelines by tradesmen, and were more often than not designed for outdoor activities, including such articles as children's swings, hoops and kites. Toymakers kept pace with new advances, such as chromolithographic printing methods, which allowed for colourful and attractive games, and also kept abreast of changing fashions and developments in society including the rising popularity of sport (67–69).

It is one of the great ironies of toymaking that games are designed by adults primarily to attract the attention of other adults, the potential money-paying customers. This helps explain why the products are often enjoyed just as much by the parents as by the intended players, the children, and why many games are targeted specifically for adults. In Victorian England there was a great emphasis on games with a strong educational theme, children learning as they play, or alternatively the so-called 'Games of Morals'. In later years, however, attitudes relaxed and it became more accepted that games could also be given to children for the sheer natural enjoyment of play.

Sport became an increasingly popular theme for the board game, although soccer presented the designer with more difficulties than other activities. The easiest sports to reproduce in this form were race games, whether horse racing, motor racing or athletics, where players could advance

66 Official international match pennants (left to right): The Hungarian Football Association pennant for the England v. Hungary international match played at Highbury, 2 December 1936; the Yugoslav Football Association pennant for the Yugoslavia v. England international match played in Belgrade, 18 May 1939; the Belgian Football Association pennant for the Belgium v. England international match played in Brussels, 21 September 1947; and the Portuguese Football Association pennant for the Portugal v. England international match played in Lisbon, 25 May 1947.

67 Football board game: 'Playing For The Cup'.

68 Blow football.

along a marked-out track with the winner determined by the simple first-past-the-post principle. The simulation of a soccer match, however, a free-flowing game, governed by rules and teamwork, was usually designed as a game of strategy, typified by a chequerboard-style playing area. This led to much competition amongst manufacturers, who would bring out new products claiming to be more 'real' and more 'exciting' than others.

There was of course a limit to this form of game, and manufacturers began turning their attentions to other methods. These included soccer card games of one description or another, but more usually actual indoor miniature simulations of soccer, requiring manual dexterity and skills, and from which some of the actual excitement of a competitive, physical sport could be artificially replicated. Blow football was a particular favourite and was produced by many different manufacturers, and then there were soccer games with miniature figures of footballers, which moved around the field of play or were used to propel the ball. Before the advent of plastic these figures were often die cast.

Of particular historical significance to many collectors are official paper ephemera relating to individual players and football clubs. For players this encompasses such items as contracts entered into with club employers, which are particularly poignant when examples are compared from different

69 Soccer table game: 'New Footy'.

periods, including the eras of the minimum and maximum wage, and of course in the context of the modern professional.

For those interested in club histories, official material surfaces from time to time. Ephemera such as directors' reports, balance sheets, share certificates, registers of shareholders, and official club correspondence can be valuable sources for historical research; especially when it can be found in a form as grand as the illustrated Bolton Wanderers articles (70), which include gate receipt books, directors' minute books and wage record ledgers, bound in large tooled leather covers.

At times of success, such as League and Cup triumphs, there has been a long tradition of clubs marking these achievements by holding celebration dinners and banquets for the families of all officials, players and other staff connected with the club. On other occasions these evenings have been held in their honour and hosted by the local mayor and civic corporation. The special menus (71) printed for these occasions, usually tied with ribbon in team colours, make for an attractive collectable, especially with their direct connection to successful times. They are frequently autographed, and can often be found complete with seating plans and ticket invitations.

Supporters' memorabilia connected with Sheffield Wednesday FC may be seen in the miscellany illustrated (72). The earliest examples relating to the

70 Official Bolton Wanderers record books

71 A selection of celebration dinner menus featuring examples from Arsenal, Wolverhampton Wanderers, Manchester United and Sheffield United

Wednesday, the fifth oldest League club, are three scarce members' tickets dating between seasons 1884–85 and 1889–90. Known more commonly now as season tickets, these items were attractively produced at this period in maroon cloth covers with gilt inscriptions, and contained the seasonal entrance pass accompanied by a list of fixtures and club rules.

There are two articles relating to the Sheffield Wednesday Supporters Club from the 1930s. The first is a dinner menu for the club's sixth annual dinner, a reunion held at a local Sheffield restaurant; the other is a souvenir item in the form of a blotter made to celebrate the team's defeat of West Bromwich Albion in the 1935 FA Cup final. This was Wednesday's third victory in the Cup.

The sounds and songs of the terraces are embodied in the song sheet for 'The Wednesday Anthem', composed in 1935 by Joseph Gillott and dedicated to Sheffield Wednesday Football Club and its supporters. 'Dear owd Wednesday's glory shall, niver, niver, niver fade!', proclaims the song's subtitle.

A 1935 gilt-metal and enamel stewards' badge, a 1950s wooden rattle painted in the team colours, and a commemorative LP recording featuring

72 A miscellany of Sheffield Wednesday supporters' memorabilia.

the 1966 Cup final encounter against Everton make up the remainder of the illustration (72) featuring the famous Yorkshire club.

Autograph hunting has always been a highly popular pursuit of soccer fans, especially schoolboys, and there is a wealth of autographed material in existence, particularly dating from the spectator boom years of the 1950s. It is the one area of soccer memorabilia where a collection can be built up from new with very little financial outlay. All that is really required is the goodwill of the players, and an abundance of enthusiasm to be in the right place at the right time. Many collectors who built up extensive autograph collections in the 1950s talk with great fondness of the times, for example, when they assembled at the main London rail terminals on Saturday mornings awaiting the arrival of teams for their scheduled matches in the capital.

There is also much surviving autographed material from the 1930s, but it becomes progressively rarer before this date. It is fascinating to see the changing styles of autographs over the years. In the team group sets from the 1930s and earlier, the players tended to autograph the page in neat columns, and the signatures were written legibly in a similar joined-up style, very much the way they had been taught at school. In the 1950s the autograph styles became increasingly idiosyncratic and were applied to the sheet in a more random manner. Today, players' autographs are very often highly personalised and it can be extremely difficult to decipher the name from the squiggles, loops and other flourishes that make up the signature.

Presentation and condition is a vital factor in autograph collecting. Autographs must be presented in an orderly, clean and desirable fashion, with the signatures crisp and unfaded. This can often be of more importance than the identities of stars whose autographs have been collected. With such a wealth of material available, collectors know that superior versions could appear at any moment.

Most autographs are found in the pages of albums and scrapbooks, but they can be more desirable when the signatures have been collected in more creative ways (illustrated p. 8). Collecting autographs on the panels of footballs is a popular method and provides a far more literal piece of soccer memorabilia. The only drawback is that the autographs are far more susceptible to condition problems, especially fading, than when gathered and protected within a closed album. Shirts, too, are a popular alternative method of displaying autographs, and the final article has a wealth of possibilities for the autographs to be seen and enjoyed. On a smaller scale this can be achieved by an autographed photograph or a bookplate, which can be simply framed and displayed.

The OFFICIAL SOUVENIR PROGRAMME

1919-20

of the
FINAL TIE
FOOTBALL ASSOCIATION
CHALLENGE CUP
COMPETITION

STAMFORD BRIDGE S.W.   APRIL 24 1920

Price Sixpence

FINAL TIE
OF THE FOOTBALL ASSOCIATION'S
ENGLISH CUP COMPETITION.

1924

IN THE STADIUM AT THE BRITISH EMPIRE EXHIBITION Wembley

PROGRAMME & SOUVENIR.
Printed and Published by Fleetway Press Ltd.

1/-

FINAL TIE

Of the Football Association
English Cup Competition
APRIL 25th, 1925

STADIUM

British Empire Exhibition
Wembley

Official Programme - 6d.

Printed and Published by Thomas Forman, 5-8, Dove Street, High Holborn, London, W.C.1

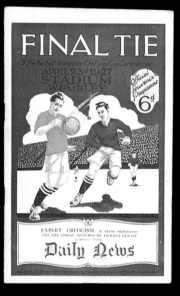

FINAL TIE
Of the Football Association Challenge Cup Competition

APRIL 23rd 1927
STADIUM
WEMBLEY

Official Souvenir Programme

6d

EXPERT CRITICISM by FRANK THOROGOOD
AND THE FINEST PICTURES OF TO-DAY'S CUP-TIE
Daily News

PRINTED & PUBLISHED BY FRED E. BLOWER, 152 HIGH STREET, WATFORD

OFFICIAL SOUVENIR PROGRAMME – SIXPENCE

FINAL TIE
of the
FOOTBALL ASSOCIATION CHALLENGE
CUP COMPETITION

April 21st 1928

WEMBLEY STADIUM

EXPERT CRITICISM
By FRANK THOROGOOD
and the finest pictures of to-day's Cup-Tie
in Monday's
Daily News & Westminster

PRODUCED & PUBLISHED BY FRED. E. BLOWER & CO, 152 HIGH ST, WATFORD

FINAL TIE

OF THE FOOTBALL ASSOCIATION CHALLENGE CUP COMPETITION

AT THE
EMPIRE STADIUM
WEMBLEY

SATURDAY · APRIL 27th · 1935

Their Majesties' Silver Jubilee Year

OFFICIAL PROGRAMME SIXPENCE

FINAL TIE

OF THE FOOTBALL ASSOCIATION CHALLENGE CUP COMPETITION

AT THE
Empire Stadium Wembley

SATURDAY, APRIL 25th, 1936

ARSENAL
v.
SHEFFIELD UNITED

Kick-off 3 p.m.

OFFICIAL PROGRAMME SIXPENCE

EMPIRE STADIUM
WEMBLEY

SATURDAY, MAY 30th, 1942

LONDON WAR CUP FINAL

PORTSMOUTH
v.
BRENTFORD

AIR RAID PRECAUTIONS

In the event of an Air Raid Alert, in the course of which information is given by the Spotters that Enemy Aircraft are in the immediate vicinity of the Stadium, an announcement will be made over the loudspeakers.
Spectators will then be requested to leave the enclosures and make their way quietly to the Circulating Corridors under the Stands, as directed by the Stewards and Officials.
Those wishing to leave the Stadium may do so by any of the usual Exits.

6d.   OFFICIAL PROGRAMME   6d.

OFFICIAL PROGRAMME
The
BOLTON WANDERERS
FOOTBALL & ATHLETIC CO., LTD.

President – Sir WILLIAM EDGE, Bart, M.P.
Directors:
Chairman : C. N. Banks   Dr. A. Cochrane   P. Danbury
E. Prestwich   Alderman J. Entwistle, J.P.   W. Haywood
E. Gerrard   H. Warburton
WALTER J. ROWLEY, Secretary-Manager

FOOTBALL LEAGUE (NORTH) CUP
FINAL TIE

Bolton Wanderers
v.
Manchester United

AT BURNDEN PARK, BOLTON
Saturday, 19th May, 1945

KICK-OFF 3-0 P.M.   PROGRAMME 2d.

Printed for the Bolton Wanderers F. & Ath. Co. Ltd. by Hilland & Harlow Ltd. 5 Bank Street, Bolton

chapter six

Match Programmes

Programmes are by far the most popular collecting category within the entire sphere of soccer memorabilia. They are also the most abundant items in the marketplace, with countless opportunities arising for collectors to acquire them.

It was also the first area of soccer memorabilia that became organised as a serious pastime in the1970s, a time when there was only limited interest in many of the other categories of collecting surveyed in this book. Early indications of this interest became evident in the 1950s when collectors began placing classified advertisements in the famous soccer magazines of the day. This eventually led to Charles Buchan's *Football Monthly* having a regular 'programme-exchange' section within the publication, and a similar feature appearing in *Soccer Star*. As collecting gathered speed, the hobby became supported by a structure of dealers, programme fairs, collectors' clubs, conventions, specialist periodicals and books, and in later times the auction houses. With this level of accessibility it is possible to build up a good knowledge of the subject quickly and take advantage of the huge availability of material.

For many fans, the programme is an integral part of the enjoyment of the game, and there can be few supporters who have not kept a few examples from the matches that they have attended over the years, with many, indeed, keeping most or all of them. It is a subject that holds a special appeal for fans, and many feel a desire to augment the programmes they have amassed through their participation as spectators with examples that can be collected from the past. As well as being enjoyable publications to own and read, their editorial matters, pictures and advertisements provide an important source of historical information and also offer valuable insight into how the game used to be in the past.

Naturally, many people concentrate on collecting match programmes connected with the clubs they support, but the subject offers a wide diversity of possibilities. There are a number of recognised

73 Examples of FA Cup final programmes dating between 1920 and 1945.

74 Walsall Town Swifts v. Preston North End match card, 27 October 1890.

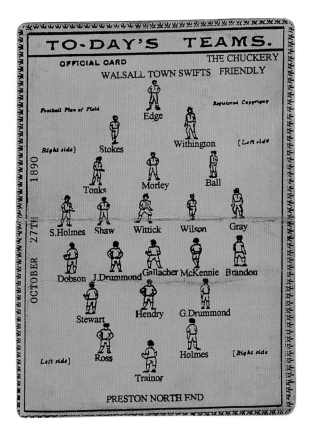

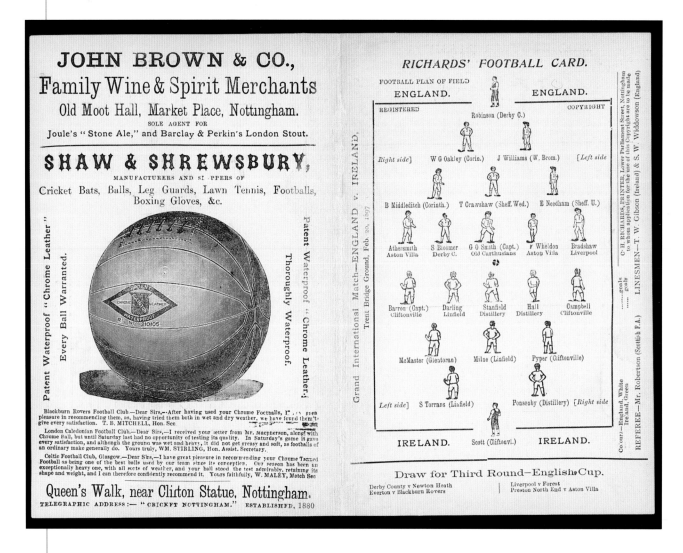

75 England v. Ireland international match card, 20 February 1897.

categories to choose from, a selection of which will be highlighted in this chapter, and of course these can be cut across to form eclectic and comprehensive collections.

The match programme has evolved a great deal over the years, and the big, glossy productions of today bear little resemblance to the examples from the formative years of the sport. It is not known when the first soccer programmes were produced, although the earliest surviving examples date from the 1870s and 1880s. The primary objective was simply to inform spectators who was playing in the day's match, and these early examples take the form of single sheet, handbill or card printed with the team line-ups, often accompanied by advertisements placed by local traders or sporting goods companies. Examples illustrated here (74 & 75) are for Walsall Swifts (formed in 1877, merged with Walsall Town in 1888, the club known simply as Walsall from 1895); and a card for the England v. Ireland international match played at Trent Bridge, Nottingham on 20 February 1897. The England card is folded at the centre, which allowed for printing and advertisements on four sides.

76 A match card for the Arthur Chadwick benefit match, Southampton v. Woolwich Arsenal, 21 November 1900.

A fairly common feature from the start was to have the team line-ups printed in their respective field positions, a tradition that in some cases has endured ever since. In these early examples, however, the line-ups were often accompanied by artist-drawn footballers in different poses, printed together with the names of the players.

A new development was the match card printed with photographic illustrations on the cover. The example from Southampton FC (76), designed as a small folded card, was produced for the Arthur Chadwick Benefit Match against Woolwich Arsenal on 21 November 1900. Chadwick won two England caps while playing for Southampton between 1897 and 1900, and is seen in a studio portrait wearing an England shirt and cap.

These early cards contained little information and were very ephemeral in nature. They are now extremely scarce and it is a miracle that many of them have survived at all. They were retained with greater frequency once they became more substantial publications, and designed as the style of programme that is more familiar to us today. The new multi-sheet programme in a larger format, typically costing a penny, contained additional information and editorial features and was more likely to be kept as a souvenir. But still, programmes are rare to find up to the First World War, which is viewed as an important historical watershed in collecting.

An indication of the growth of interest in match programmes is evident from the number of bound volumes that began to emerge in this period.

Programmes were becoming an increasingly lucrative source of income for clubs, and many including Aston Villa, Chelsea, Sheffield United and others offered sets of match programmes to supporters covering a full season, preserved in protective bindings. Many of the programmes that have survived from this date have been removed from bound volumes.

From the inter-war period, League programmes come in a variety of sizes and formats from club to club (77). Also clubs often revised the design of their match programmes. Colour printing became a more popular feature, and the choice of colour for the paper also began to vary to a greater degree. The prices of these programmes were usually a penny or tuppence.

For many years the front covers of Tottenham Hotspur match programmes featured a cartoon mascot known as 'Cocky' the Cockerel. From week to week he could be seen inflicting some ghastly fate upon the visiting team and its supporters, in a fashion that would have raised many eyebrows in later, more contentious times. The present example portrays 'Cocky' as a barber cutting off the ear of Blackburn's 'Rover' with his razor and popping it into a box labelled 'League Points'. Chelsea's match programme, called the *Chelsea FC Chronicle* also had cartoon covers, sometimes featuring 'The Chelsea Pensioners'.

The Sheffield Wednesday programme is for the match against Arsenal on 7 September 1929 and is interesting as it is an example of a VIP edition, a type that would have been issued to club directors or their guests. The programme is bound in outer card covers and tied with ribbon in the blue and white colours of the club. The example from Wednesday's great rivals Sheffield United is a black-edged memorial programme for a match commemorating the late Joe Nicholson in 1932. Nicholson was the 'Blades' club secretary and had been expected to join the team to travel to Birmingham by rail for a match before it was discovered that he had tragically committed suicide by dashing in front of a lorry.

The programmes produced for FA Cup finals (73) are an extremely popular field of collecting. In many cases an individual's interest may extend to semi-finals, and even earlier rounds. Very few early examples from Cup finals are known to exist, and those that have surfaced are extremely rare and take the form of simple printed team sheets. They appear with a little greater frequency from the Crystal Palace period (1895–1914) onwards, but programmes predating the finals played at the newly built Empire Stadium at Wembley in 1923 are scarce.

Between 1920 and 1922 the final ties were played at Stamford Bridge, and illustrated is a programme for the first of these Cup finals between Aston Villa and Huddersfield Town, costing a whopping sixpence; its cover is illustrated with a winged figure of Victory presiding over the FA Cup trophy, while to either side of her, two classical columns are inscribed with the names

77 A selection of pre-war match programmes.

of the previous winners of the competition. By 1924 and the second of the Wembley finals, the supporters of Aston Villa and Newcastle United were required to pay a shilling for the match programme, which had colourful pictorial covers. It appears to have been conceded that this was too expensive, and the price reverted to sixpence and remained so until the Second World War. The covers of the 1924 programme were printed on paper inferior in quality to the rest of the programme. Consequently, they have become detached from many copies, making the complete programme a rare and desirable item.

The designs of the covers changed annually until the war, and a number of examples are illustrated here. During the war, with paper rationing introduced, all programmes had to be restricted in size and format, not excluding those produced for the regional Wartime Cup competitions held between 1940 and 1945.

The availability of FA Cup final programmes to collectors becomes far greater in the postwar era. To the one shilling examples from the 1950s (78) can be compared the Cup final oversize programme that has been introduced in recent times. The 1993 programme, between Arsenal and Sheffield Wednesday, was produced with a hologram on the cover and the cost had spiralled to five pounds. The illustration also contains examples of other British finals that attract many collectors, and comprises Scottish Cup finals and Scottish and English League Cup finals, including those competitions endorsed in recent times by sponsors.

A distinct collecting area is wartime soccer. Because many of these programmes were produced as ephemeral single sheets, they were very likely to have been discarded. At some grounds, in fact, fans were encouraged to deposit their programmes after matches into special waste bins, so that the paper could be recycled to help the war effort. Programmes from this period are made even rarer today by the fact that crowds were of course much smaller than in peacetime.

During hostilities, players' contracts were suspended and they could therefore make guest appearances for any clubs they chose. Many of the leading players of the day were still in demand and played a good deal of soccer in this period. They were also often serving in the Army in the capacity of physical fitness instructors and similar positions.

Interest in this field for collectors can simply mean an extension of other programme categories such as clubs or Cup finals, and then it is simply a question of hunting down these more elusive examples. On the other hand, wartime soccer offers many programmes representing the special matches that were staged largely as morale boosting exercises of public entertainment. Many of these games involved various branches of the armed forces, and other organisations connected to Britain's civil defence. Single sheets from

OFFICIAL PROGRAMME

Scottish

CUP FINAL

RANGERS (HOLDERS) v CELTIC

HAMPDEN PARK, MAY 4, 1963   KICK-OFF 3 P.M.

OFFICIAL PROGRAMME

SCOTTISH LEAGUE CUP

CELTIC
versus
PARTICK THISTLE

KICK-OFF — 2.15 p.m.

FINAL
HAMPDEN PARK
SATURDAY
OCTOBER 27th, 1956

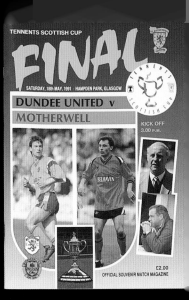

TENNENTS SCOTTISH CUP

FINAL

SATURDAY, 18th MAY, 1991 · HAMPDEN PARK, GLASGOW

DUNDEE UNITED v MOTHERWELL

KICK OFF 3.00 P.M.

£2.00

OFFICIAL SOUVENIR MATCH MAGAZINE

OFFICIAL PROGRAMME

Scottish Cup Final

CELTIC v. CLYDE

HAMPDEN PARK
APRIL 23 KICK-OFF
1955   3 P.M.

PRICE
6D

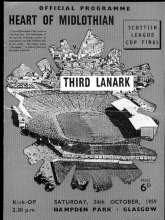

OFFICIAL PROGRAMME

HEART OF MIDLOTHIAN

SCOTTISH
LEAGUE
CUP FINAL

THIRD LANARK

Kick-Off
2.30 p.m.

SATURDAY, 24th OCTOBER, 1959

HAMPDEN PARK · GLASGOW

PRICE
6D

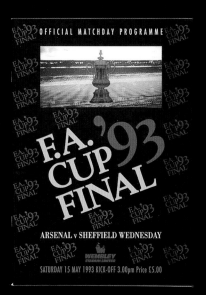

OFFICIAL MATCHDAY PROGRAMME

F.A. '93 CUP FINAL

ARSENAL v SHEFFIELD WEDNESDAY

WEMBLEY
STADIUM LIMITED

SATURDAY 15 MAY 1993 KICK-OFF 3.00pm Price £5.00

THE FOOTBALL ASSOCIATION CHALLENGE CUP COMPETITION

FINAL TIE

BOLTON WANDERERS
V
MANCHESTER UNITED

SATURDAY, MAY 3rd, 1958   KICK-OFF 3 pm

EMPIRE STADIUM
WEMBLEY

OFFICIAL PROGRAMME   ·   ONE SHILLING

THE FOOTBALL LEAGUE

CUP FINAL

QUEEN'S PARK RANGERS
VERSUS
WEST BROMWICH ALBION
(HOLDERS)

SATURDAY MARCH 4th, 1967
Kick-off 3.30 p.m.

EMPIRE
STADIUM WEMBLEY

OFFICIAL PROGRAMME — ONE SHILLING

Incorporating Special Cup Final Issue of Football League Review

BLUES News

THE OFFICIAL PROGRAMME OF
BIRMINGHAM CITY
FOOTBALL CLUB

SEASON 1962-63   ·   PRICE FOURPENCE

THE FOOTBALL ASSOCIATION CHALLENGE CUP COMPETITION
FINAL TIE
Arsenal v Liverpool
SATURDAY, APRIL 29th, 1950 at 3 pm

OFFICIAL PROGRAMME · ONE SHILLING

The Empire Stadium
WEMBLEY

THE 100th YEAR OF THE WORLD'S OLDEST LEAGUE

Littlewoods
HOME SHOPPING · STORES

CHALLENGE CUP · FINAL

ARSENAL v LUTON TOWN

KICK-OFF 2.30pm · 24 APRIL 1988

OFFICIAL
SOUVENIR · PROGRAMME   WEMBLEY

both these collecting interests are illustrated (79), including a number of games staged at Portsmouth FC with its close proximity to the important Naval base. For similar reasons Aldershot became another important footballing centre.

The Tottenham Hotspur v. Cardiff City programme from the League War Cup of 1941 is printed with advice under the heading Air Raid Shelter. 'In the event of an Air Raid Warning being received the Police will instruct the Referee to stop the game when they deem it necessary and the players will leave the field. Spectators must take shelter and remain under cover until the "All Clear" has been given.'

In 1942 Brighton & Hove Albion were able to maintain the normal multi-paged format of their programme by reducing its size to almost miniature proportions.

Many collectors try to obtain programmes for matches of special importance or significance. These may include, for example, programmes representing defunct or ex-League clubs, the opening of a ground or a stand, inaugural floodlit matches, a record crowd attendance, a player's testimonial, and other specially arranged games.

International matches (80) provide another popular area of programme-collecting. England played their first match at Wembley in 1924 against Scotland, but the stadium did not become their permanent home until the 1950s. It was used exclusively as an international stage for the encounters between the 'auld enemies' until 9 May 1951, when Argentina became the first team other than Scotland to face England at Wembley, in a friendly match held in conjunction with the Festival of Britain.

The pre war programmes for the England v. Scotland matches often had colourful pictorial covers, such as the illustrated 1932 example, but from the late 1940s onwards they were smaller and had similar designs to those for the Wembley Cup finals, typified by covers printed in muted shades of green and blue. Also illustrated are examples of Scotland and Northern Ireland international homes, and away programmes, which are considerably rarer to find in Britain. The Swiss programme for the match against Scotland in 1957 is particularly stylish, while the 1969 Netherlands programme for the match against England portrays a boys' comic-style illustration of a Dutch footballer.

In recent times UEFA (Union of European Football Association) and FIFA have made it compulsory for programmes to be produced for all international and European competition matches. In earlier times programme production for these matches was far more sporadic from country to country.

There is also much interest in programmes produced for matches that had to be postponed, many of which are extremely difficult to find. An extension to this 'Game that never was' principle is represented by the

78 (previous page) A selection of English and Scottish post-war FA Cup and League Cup final programmes.

79 Programmes for wartime soccer fixtures.

MANCHESTER UNITED
OFFICIAL PROGRAMME PRICE 1'
FIXTURES FOR SEASON—1946-47

MATCHES PLAYED AT MAINE ROAD. LEAGUE TEAM FIXTURES	MATCHES PLAYED AT OLD TRAFFORD. CENTRAL LEAGUE FIXTURES

NEXT MATCH:
Manchester United Reserves v. Bury Reserves
At OLD TRAFFORD on SATURDAY, 30th NOVEMBER, 1946 at 2.15 p.m.

RN Y RM XI   Y FOOTBALL ASSOCIATION XI

PORTSMOUTH
FOOTBALL CLUB
OFFICIAL PROGRAMME :: TWO-PENCE

MEMBERS OF THE FOOTBALL LEAGUE DIV. 1

PRESIDENT
Field Marshal The Viscount Montgomery of Alamein, G.C.B., D.S.O.

BOARD OF DIRECTORS

Royal Navy & Royal Marines XI
versus
Football Association XI
Wednesday, February 26th, 1947
Wednesday, December 11th, 1946

SPARSHATTS
Dennis Leyland Dodge
COMMERCIAL VEHICLE DISTRIBUTORS

CHELSEA FOOTBALL CLUB
Official Programme
SATURDAY MAY 20th 1944   PRICE ONE PENNY

ASTON VILLA v. CHARLTON ATHLETIC
IN AID OF KING GEORGE'S FUND FOR SAILORS   Kick-off 2.45 p.m.

ASTON VILLA (Claret and Light Blue)

Referee—Mr. G. READER (Hants.)

CHARLTON ATHLETIC (Red)

KING GEORGE'S FUND FOR SAILORS

WAR SAVINGS CENTRE, 8, THE BROADWAY, WALHAM GREEN for your Stamps and Certificates.

PORTSMOUTH
FOOTBALL CLUB

MEMBERS OF THE FOOTBALL LEAGUE DIV. 1

PROGRAMME - PRICE 2d.

INTER-COMMAND CUP COMPETITION FINAL TIE

PORTSMOUTH COMMAND
versus
HOME AIR COMMAND

Wednesday, March 31st, 1948
Kick-off 3 p.m.

BIJOU PROGRAMME . . . . . TWO-PENCE

BRIGHTON & HOVE ALBION
FOOTBALL CLUB

Crosse & Blackwell
Quality Foods

Tottenham Hotspur Football & Athletic Company, Limited.
OFFICIAL PROGRAMME.
MARCH 22nd, 1941.   Price:- ONE PENNY.

LEAGUE WAR CUP.
On Saturday, March 29th,
ARSENAL v. WEST HAM
Kick-off 3.0 p.m.

League War Cup   Sat. Mar. 22nd, 1941.   Kick-off 3.0 p.m.
TOTTENHAM HOTSPUR
White Shirts, Blue Knickers

RIGHT WING   LEFT WING

Referee—Mr. G. DUTTON
Linesmen—Mr. E. PRATT (Blue and White Flag)
Mr. F. W. CLARK (Red and White Flag)

LEFT WING   RIGHT WING
CARDIFF CITY
Shirts: Royal Blue & White Knickers

ANY ALTERATION WILL BE NOTED ON THE BOARD.

AIR RAID SHELTER.
In the event of an Air Raid Warning being received the Police will instruct the Referee to stop the game when they deem it necessary and the players will leave the field. Spectators must take shelter and remain under cover until the "All Clear" has been given.

Will patrons please refrain from changing their positions and going from behind one Goal to the other?

PORTSMOUTH
FOOTBALL CLUB

MEMBERS OF THE FOOTBALL LEAGUE DIV. 1

OFFICIAL PROGRAMME :: TWO-PENCE

PRESIDENT
Field Marshal The Viscount Montgomery of Alamein, G.C.B., D.S.O.

BOARD OF DIRECTORS:

NAVY CUP FINAL

ROYAL MARINES
(Portsmouth)
versus
ROYAL MARINES
(Chatham)

SPARSHATTS
Dennis Leyland Dodge
COMMERCIAL VEHICLE DISTRIBUTORS

PORTSMOUTH
FOOTBALL CLUB

MEMBERS OF THE FOOTBALL LEAGUE DIV. 1

OFFICIAL PROGRAMME :: TWO-PENCE

Souvenir Programme
PRICE 2d.

F.A. XI
versus
Combined Services XI

Wednesday, 12th December, 1945
Kick-off 2.15 p.m.

CHELSEA FOOTBALL CLUB
Official Programme
SATURDAY APRIL 29th 1944   PRICE ONE PENNY

ENGLAND XI 3 v. COMBINED SERVICES XI
Kick-off 3 p.m.

ENGLAND XI (White)

Referee—Mr. C. E. ARGENT (Herts.)

COMBINED SERVICES XI (Red)

TODAYS GAME IS IN AID OF SERVICE CHARITIES

WAR SAVINGS CENTRE, 8, THE BROADWAY, WALHAM GREEN for your Stamps and Certificates.

80 A selection of international match programmes.

81 A game that never was: a programme produced in the event of a replay for the 1971 FA Cup final.

Arsenal v. Liverpool Cup final replay programme (81). This rare item was produced in readiness for the event of a replay being required to settle the 1971 FA Cup final. The replay was scheduled for just three days later at Hillsborough, and there would not have been enough time to produce a programme from scratch. Charlie George's winning goal for Arsenal deep into extra time meant that the replay programme was never required and never officially published.

REPLAY

F.A. CUP FINAL '71

ARSENAL
V
LIVERPOOL

At Hillsborough, Sheffield
Tuesday, 11th May, 1971
Kick-off 7-45 p.m.

PRICE 10P
Official Programme

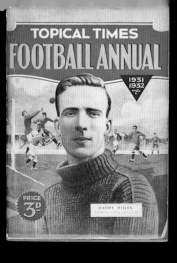

TOPICAL TIMES
FOOTBALL ANNUAL
1931-1932

PRICE 3D

HARRY HIBBS
BIRMINGHAM & ENGLAND

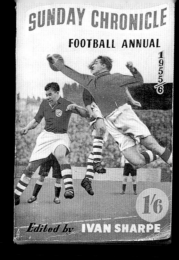

SUNDAY CHRONICLE
FOOTBALL ANNUAL
1955/6

1/6

Edited by **IVAN SHARPE**

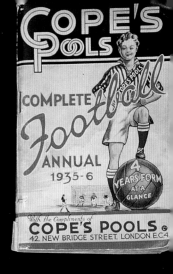

COPE'S POOLS

COMPLETE
Football
ANNUAL
1935-6

4 YEARS FORM AT A GLANCE

With the Compliments of
COPE'S POOLS
42, NEW BRIDGE STREET, LONDON, E.C.4

FINDON'S
FOOTBALL
HANDBOOK 1946-7
100 PAGES ONE SHILLING

ENGLISH, IRISH
AND SCOTTISH
FIXTURES
• • •
Winning Hints for
POOL PUNTERS
• • •
TEAMS TO FOLLOW
• • •
Exclusive Articles
by Famous Football
Writers and Stars
including
LESLIE SMITH
JOE MERCER
• • •
EVERYTHING THE
SOCCER FAN WANTS
TO KNOW

A FINDON PUBLICATION

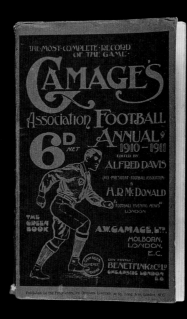

THE MOST COMPLETE RECORD OF THE GAME
GAMAGE'S
Association Football
6D NET **ANNUAL**
1910-1911
EDITED BY
ALFRED DAVIS
(VICE-PRESIDENT FOOTBALL ASSOCIATION)
&
A.R. McDONALD
"FOOTBALL EVENING NEWS"
LONDON

THE GREEN BOOK

A.W. GAMAGE, LTD.
HOLBORN,
LONDON,
E.C.
CITY BRANCH:
BENETFINK & CO. LTD
CHEAPSIDE LONDON E.C.

Published for the Proprietors by OPHAMS LIMITED, 34-40, Long Acre, London, W.C.

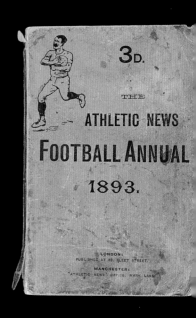

3D.

THE
ATHLETIC NEWS
FOOTBALL ANNUAL
1893.

LONDON:
PUBLISHED AT 65, FLEET STREET.
MANCHESTER:
"ATHLETIC NEWS" OFFICE. MARK LANE.

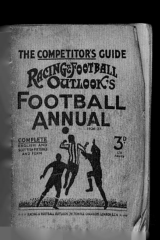

THE COMPETITOR'S GUIDE
RACING & FOOTBALL
OUTLOOK'S
FOOTBALL
ANNUAL
1926-27

COMPLETE
ENGLISH AND
SCOTTISH FIXTURES
AND FORM

3D

RACING & FOOTBALL OUTLOOK 79, TEMPLE CHAMBERS LONDON E.C.4

2D **Daily News**
(NORTHERN EDITION)

1920-21

FOOTBALL
ANNUAL

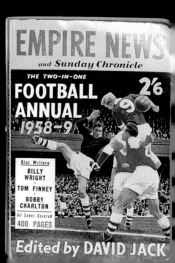

EMPIRE NEWS
and Sunday Chronicle
THE TWO-IN-ONE
FOOTBALL
ANNUAL
1958-9

2/6

Star Writers
BILLY WRIGHT
TOM FINNEY
BOBBY CHARLTON
All Codes Covered
400 PAGES

Edited by **DAVID JACK**

chapter seven

Books and Publications

For any collector wishing to concentrate on soccer publications, Peter J. Seddon's *A Football Compendium* (The British Library National Bibliographic Service, 1995, revised and published, 2000) is essential. This authoritative guide attempted with great success to compile an exhaustive listing of soccer publications primarily from 1863 (the year of the formation of the FA) to the time of publishing, and consists of over 5,000 entries. Very rarely does a work surface so scarce that it has evaded the compiler's attention.

In many ways soccer literature has mirrored the development of the sport itself. Much of the contemporaneous writing on the game's prehistory is scathing about it, and pulls few punches in its vitriolic criticism of the sport. Then from the Grand Amateur Era the first seminal works begin to emerge, with a number of fine reminiscences written by those with direct involvement in the game's greater degree of organisation in the late Victorian and Edwardian years, the authors often drawing on their experiences as players as well as administrators. Famous contributors from the period include personalities already discussed in this book, such as Charles Alcock, author of *Football: Our Winter Game* (Field, 1874), and Nicholas Lane 'Pa' Jackson, chief contributor to the 412-page *Association Football* (G. Newnes, 1899) (84). Two important early histories are Montague Shearman's *Athletics and Football* (Longmans, Green & Co., 1887) (83) in the Badminton Library series and James A. H. Catton's *The Real Football: a sketch of the development of the association game* (Sands, 1900)(84).

These books were often expensive and lavishly produced, reflecting the social status of both the authors and the interested readership of this period. The epitome of this era of literature was Gibson and Pickford's classic *Association Football & The Men Who Made It* (Caxton, 1905–06), published in four volumes, each containing over 200 pages, with its famous blue illustrated cover designed by the artist John Hassall. It is remarkable for its scope of subject-matter and an essential historical work (83).

Other notable works include *The Book of Football* (Amalgamated Press, 1906), which was originally published in twelve fortnightly parts and written by a number of contributors; and *Cricket and Football* (British Sports and Sportsmen, 1917) (83), edited and compiled by 'The Sportsman' of *The Sporting Life*, and perhaps the most lavish of them all. This heavy tome bound between leather boards, featuring about seventy pages on Association Football, was published in two limited editions of 1,000 copies, comprising the deluxe version bound in red leather and the alternative version in green cloth.

82 A selection of famous football annuals.

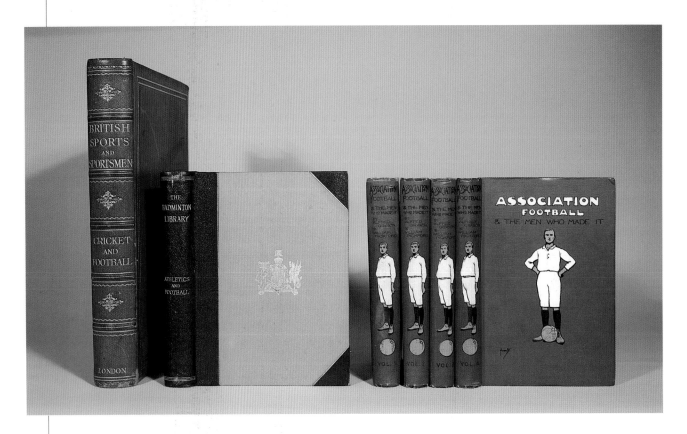

At this same time a number of publications devoted to the theory and practice of soccer began to emerge, beginning a tradition that was to develop in future years as coaching, tactics, training, athleticism and fitness gained greater emphasis. The early works improved with each publication and reached a landmark with Evers and Davies' *The Complete Association Footballer* (Methuen, 1912)(85), a work already encountered in earlier chapters here, and representing the first truly comprehensive examination of its subject.

With the greater withdrawal of the gentleman soccer enthusiast after the Great War, the opulence of publications lessened. Now the game was firmly back in the domain of the working man who, even if he had the inclination, had precious little disposable income to satisfy his literary interests. As a consequence, the commercial possibilities for publishers became far more limited. Some of the more significant publications from the interwar years include James A.H. Catton's *Wickets and Goals: Stories of Play* (Chapman & Hall, 1926) (85), the works of Charles Buchan (the former Sunderland and Arsenal player), an anecdotal collaboration titled *The Mighty Kick* (Jarrolds, 1933) (85), and *The Story of the Football League* (Football League, 1938)(85), compiled by Sutcliffe, Brierley and Howarth, a fine work celebrating the League's golden anniversary.

Just as crowds returned to matches in record numbers in the immediate postwar period, so the number of soccer publications began to mushroom to unprecedented levels. The range of books became more far reaching, and began to cover specialised study as well as providing new and enlightening overviews of the sport. The writing itself also varied between scholarly sociological examinations and outright humorous entertainment and trivia.

Modern masters include Geoffrey Green, whose numerous works include his monumental *The History of the Football Association* (Naldrett, 1953) (86); Brian Glanville whose output is too prolific to do justice here, but includes *Soccer Nemesis* (Secker & Warburg, 1955)(86), which caused something of a sensation when it was published in the wake of England's historic defeat by Hungary, and praises the qualities of foreign soccer while criticising the state of the British game in equal measure. In recent times Simon Inglis has produced a number of books remarkable for their impeccably researched and scholarly approach, none more so perhaps than *League Football and the Men Who Made It* (Willow, 1988) (86).

Another feature of the post-war period has been the emergence of the club history. The earlier attempts in this field were often ephemeral in nature, such as pamphlets and handbooks, some of the notable exceptions being Richard Robinson's *History of the Queen's Park Football Club, 1867–1917* (Hay Nisbet, 1920), (85) Charles Francis's *History of the Blackburn Rovers, 1875–1925* (Toulmin, 1925), (85) John

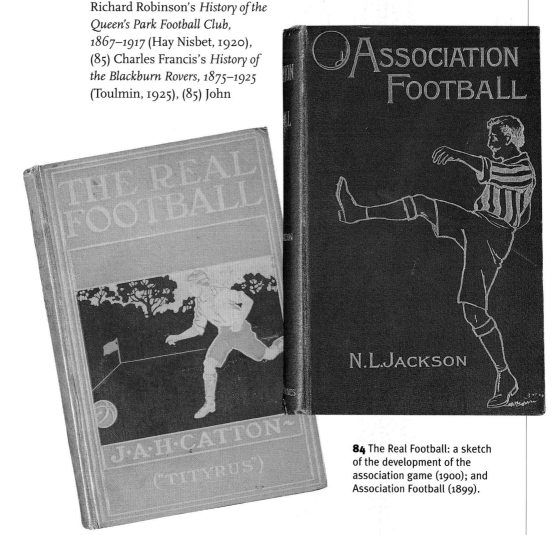

84 The Real Football: a sketch of the development of the association game (1900); and Association Football (1899).

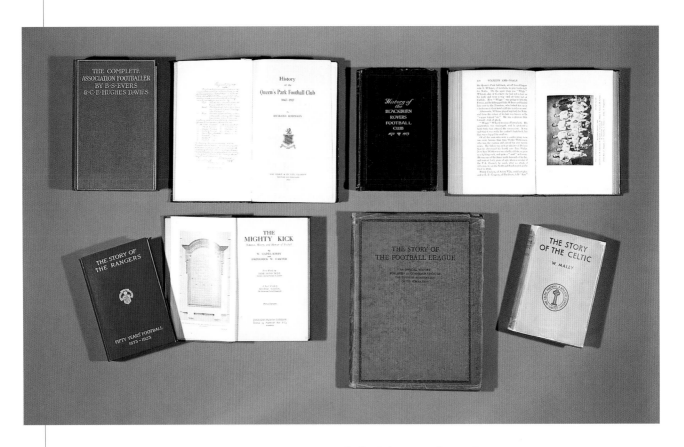

Allan's *The Story of Rangers, 1873–1923* (Rangers Football Club, 1923) (85) and Willie Maley's *The Story of Celtic* (Villafield, 1939) (85). However, these were some of the exceptions, and to obtain a truer picture one need look no further than Manchester United FC. In 1995 Seddon listed 85 club histories on United, 37 more than on any other British club. However, the first literary attempt did not appear until 1946 – Tom Morgan's *Let's Talk About Manchester United Football Club* (Sentinel), a fairly sketchy, handbook-style publication.

This was one of a whole series of *Let's Talk About ...* Sentinel titles by Morgan, and others of its type were to follow before more substantial works began to appear on the market, Glanville again featuring prominently with the 133-page *Arsenal Football Club* (Convoy, 1952)(86). The genre expanded greatly in the 1970s and 1980s, with many clubs celebrating their centenaries, and this was followed by titles inspired by the work of organisations, such as the Association of Football Statisticians. Club histories could now be accompanied by detailed statistical summaries, thereby providing a comprehensive history and record of a given club. Additionally, and in their own right, these developments led to the publication of a number of authoritative statistical reference books and encyclopedias, including the

85 Top (left-to-right): *The Complete Association Footballer* (1912); *History of the Queen's Park Football Club* (1920); *History of the Blackburn Rovers* (1925); and *Wickets and Goals: Stories of Play* (1926).

Bottom (left-to-right): *The Story of Rangers* (1923); *The Mighty Kick* (1933); The *Story of the Football League* (1938); and *The Story of Celtic* (1939).

86 Books
Top (left-to-right):
They Kidnapped Stanley Matthews (1950); *How Steeple Sinderby Wanderers won the FA Cup* (1975); *Arsenal Football Club* (1952).

Middle (left-to-right):
The History of the Football Association (1953). *Soccer Nemesis* (1955); *Bristol Rovers: a complete record 1883–1987* (1987).

Bottom (left-to-right):
League Football and the Men Who Made It (1988); and *The Lads in Blue: the complete history of Carlisle United FC* (1995).

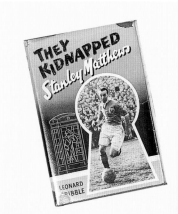
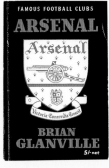
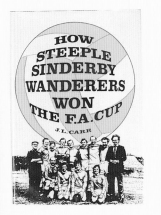
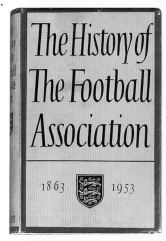
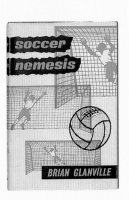

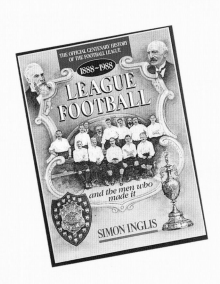
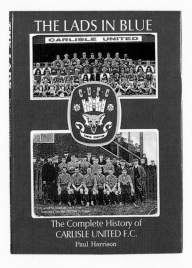

Breedon Books and Yore Publications series, the examples illustrated being Mike Jay's *Bristol Rovers: a complete record 1883–1987* (Breedon Books, 1987) (86), and Paul Harrison's *The Lads in Blue: the complete history of Carlisle United FC* (Yore Publications, 1995) (86).

The 1950s witnessed a plethora of biographies and autobiographies – accounts of the stars of the period and the memoirs of famous players of the past. The genre quickly grew in popularity readers being enthralled by the first-hand personal insight into the lives and professional careers of their footballing heroes. Players themselves soon became aware of the commercial possibilities of such books, and a multitude of footballers of widely ranging abilities soon became the focus of the written word. In recent years publishers have been launching such books with ever greater urgency, and at times when a player is very much still in mid career. Although entertaining and highly popular, the genre cannot be said to offer any serious or authoritative reflections upon a career or a life.

Another phenomenon of the modern age has been the growth of the sociological-style soccer book, where the author's primary objective is to examine the impact the game has had on people's lives, and how deeply embedded soccer has become in popular culture. Many of these works inevitably focus on the ritualised behaviour of fans, and the authorities' attempts to curb such patterns when it spills into hooliganism. Many, however, highlight the sheer pleasure of supporting a football club and watching the game, while others focus on the culture of the soccer fan in whatever way it manifests itself including, I suppose, collecting 'soccer memorabilia'. Nick Hornby's *Fever Pitch* (Victor Gollancz, 1992) must be mentioned here, a highly original, highly engaged study of football and obsession, the clear motivation of the fan; the book caught the imagination of a wide public and became a bestseller.

Unsurprisingly, with the sport's mass appeal, many attempts have been made to incorporate soccer into the plot of a novel, either as a central theme or as a background to events as they unfold. However, successful examples are few and far between, and even some of the better attempts suffer from unintentionally comic titles, such as Leonard Gribble's *They Kidnapped Stanley Matthews* (Herbert Jenkins, 1950) (86); while others, certainly not without merit, are straight from the 'Roy of the Rovers' school, such as James L. Carr's *How Steeple Sinderby Wanderers won the FA Cup* (London Magazine Editions, 1975) (86).

Largely factual soccer yearbooks or annuals (82) and other similar directories and guides began to be published from the game's formative years. They typically present club-by-club details together with current fixtures and results from the previous season, in a conveniently sized format. Publications of this kind sprouted up quickly and were often published by

87 Modern soccer annuals.

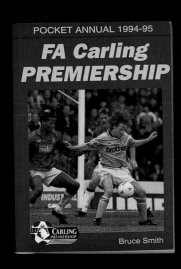

POCKET ANNUAL 1994-95
FA Carling PREMIERSHIP

Bruce Smith

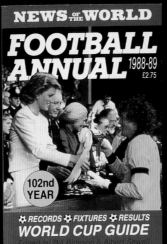

NEWS OF THE WORLD FOOTBALL ANNUAL 1988-89 £2.75

102nd YEAR

RECORDS · FIXTURES · RESULTS
WORLD CUP GUIDE
Edited by Bill Bateson & Albert Sewell

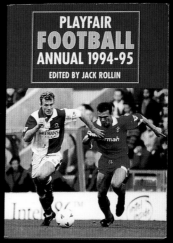

PLAYFAIR FOOTBALL ANNUAL 1994-95
EDITED BY JACK ROLLIN

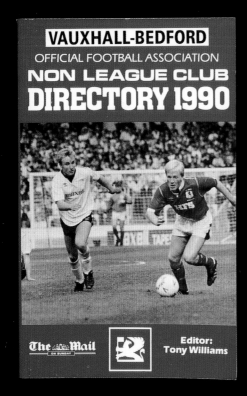

VAUXHALL-BEDFORD
OFFICIAL FOOTBALL ASSOCIATION
NON LEAGUE CLUB DIRECTORY 1990

The Mail ON SUNDAY

Editor: Tony Williams

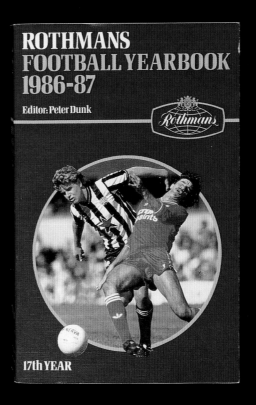

ROTHMANS FOOTBALL YEARBOOK 1986-87
Editor: Peter Dunk

Rothmans

17th YEAR

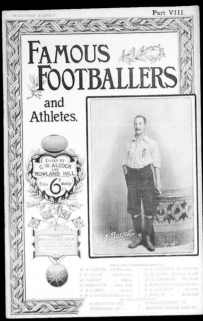

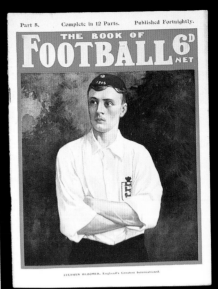

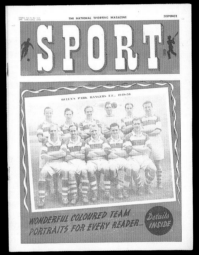

newspaper groups. The forerunner of them all was Charles William Alcock's *The Football Annual*, first published in 1872, the year the FA Cup competition was inaugurated. Its first commercial competitor came in the form of the *Sporting Chronicle Annual* which was launched by the famous sporting journal in 1876, while in Scotland a similar annual was produced by the Scottish Football Association in 1885.

The most successful of the early yearbooks, however, was the *Athletic News Football Annual*, first published in 1887. The *Athletic News* itself was published every Monday, with extensive match reports from the previous weekend's fixtures, and had a wide and enthusiastic readership. This enthusiasm transferred directly to the new annuals, which became known as soccer's equivalent of the *Wisden Cricketers' Almanack*. Its existence has been virtually unceasing, although the title has changed a number of times; it has been known as *The News of the World Annual* since 1965.

The *Gamage's Association Football Annuals*, published between 1909 and 1929, are regarded as the finest yearbooks of the period. They were far more substantial volumes than their contemporary rivals, and contained hundreds of pages packed with an array of footballing information. There were many other similar publications, often produced on a regional basis or by smaller independent publishers, in a highly competitive market that continued to produce new titles after the war (87).

Famous post-war titles include the *Playfair Football Annuals* series, first published in 1948–49, and the key publication, *Rothman's Football Yearbook*, which commenced in 1970. Rothman's was designed along the lines of the earlier *Gamage's* format, and was on quite a different scale from its pocket-sized rivals, typically containing something approaching 1,000 pages with coverage of the English, Scottish and international game. In his foreword to the first edition Sir Stanley Rous, President of FIFA, expressed a hope that it would become soccer's answer to *Wisden*. In many respects it is fair to say that this has proved true, and it is unrivalled as the foremost soccer yearbook of the modern era. The wide coverage of the sport in this format today extends to non-league football, with good quality official annuals and directories on offer for interested supporters.

Another area of publishing with a lengthy history is the football periodical or magazine (88), with the winning formula of good writing supported by lavish illustrations. These proved to be particularly popular after the Second World War, but there were many earlier examples.

The highly illustrated *Famous Footballers and Athletes*, published by Hudson & Kearns in association with *The News of the World* in 1895 in fourteen parts, contained a total of 224 numbered plates. The term 'footballer' at this period encompassed both rugby and soccer players, who received equal attention in this publication. Another early example was the

88 Football magazines and periodicals dating between 1895 and 1958.

previously discussed *The Book of Football*, which was later published in book form. It is particularly attractive to collectors when found in its original loose, twelve-part form with splendid pictorial colour covers. Sometimes the parts can be found bound together with the colour covers removed, but preserved together at the end of the volume.

In the inter-war years a number of famous titles came into being, including the popular *The Topical Times,* published in newspaper-style format every Friday. This particular publication also produced a number of supplementary souvenirs including its famous soccer picture cards, as well as its soccer annuals.

An early example of player endorsement was the magazine *Raich Carter's Soccer Star*, which bore the name of the legendary Sunderland, Derby County and England internationalist of the 1930s and 1940s. Although Carter's name was eventually dropped from the title, it endured for a long period after the war as *Soccer Star*. Another famous Sunderland and England star, Charles Buchan, made a very successful transition from footballer to journalist and author. Originally he was the soccer and golf correspondent of the *Daily News* (later amalgamated into the News Chronicle), and later a soccer commentator for the BBC. In September 1951 he became editor of the newly launched and highly popular *Football Monthly* with its famous colour covers and profuse plates, which provided favourite displays for young autograph hunters.

Sport and *Sports Reporter* were just two more of the prolific number of titles on offer to enthusiastic fans in the post-war period.

The greater internationalisation of the sport after the war inspired new titles such as *World Sports*, which had a good football coverage, and the more specific title *World Soccer*, which quickly built a fine reputation for the breadth of its international content. The domestic scene was still well catered for with such familiar titles as *Goal*, later incorporated into *Shoot*, and other weekly magazines such as *90 Minutes*.

Individual clubs have long seen the commercial opportunities in producing official souvenir publications, or authorising such works in conjunction with others. Some clubs began to produce official handbooks as an extension to match programmes long ago at the start of each season, while supporters' clubs often produced similar publications. Over the years these evolved from simple fixture lists to more substantial works giving a more detailed overview of the team's season, with editorial matter from officials, illustrations of players and managers, and statistical reviews.

The Tottenham Hotspur souvenirs illustrated (89) include an interesting selection of handbooks and other publications such as *Spurs in Action*, approved by the club and published by the *Weekly Herald* in celebration of its European success in season 1962–63. *The Lilywhite* was produced by the fans for the fans, as confirmed by its subtitle 'The official organ of the Spurs

89 A miscellany of Tottenham Hotspur Books, publications and ephemera of the 1950s and '60s.

Supporters Club', and could be said to be an innocent forerunner of the modern fanzine, lacking, of course, the irreverence typical of the latter genre. Fans could augment all of these works with a variety of other material available including souvenir newspapers, magazines and supplementary photographs, and the multitude of club-themed books that were being commissioned with ever greater frequency.

chapter eight

The 1966 World Cup

When Alf Ramsey became manager of England in 1963, ending a highly successful spell at Ipswich Town, he predicted bravely in an interview with a local Suffolk reporter: 'England will win the 1966 World Cup.' Similar fighting talk was necessary at the end of normal time of the World Cup final itself, after West Germany had scored a last-minute equalising goal. 'You've beaten them once,' he told his exhausted players, 'now you've got to do it again.' In the following thirty minutes of high drama, Geoff Hurst scored perhaps the most disputed goal in World Cup final history before completing the first and, so far, only hat trick in a World Cup final. The Boys of 66 had fulfilled Ramsey's prophecy.

The triumphant scenes that followed were unforgettable. Even today, and over three decades later, England fans speak with great fondness of the enduring images of Bobby Moore wiping his hands to shake hands with Her Majesty The Queen, Bobby Charlton's tears of joy, Nobby Stiles' victory jig, and the captain lifted by his team mates while holding aloft the Jules Rimet Trophy.

With no further comparable success for the England side, interest in this historic occasion remains undiminished. This same enthusiasm informs the area of memorabilia, with any item connected to the event eagerly sought after. Indeed, many collections are themed specifically to the 1966 World Cup, or it at least forms the keystone of a collector's wider interest. The whole World Cup tournament, the first to be held on home soil, also provided another interesting landmark. This was the first occasion that the British public had been exposed to the full commercial forces of soccer merchandising, with a huge variety of official souvenirs made available for sale.

To ensure that all the necessary arrangements for the tournament could be met in full, the FA took the decision to create the World Cup Organisation (WCO), who would report through the Secretary of the Football Association to the FA World Cup Organising Committee. The work of the WCO was coordinated by the Chief Administrative Officer and operations began at their headquarters at the White City Stadium in September 1963. The man the FA appointed as the Chief Administrative Officer of the WCO was Mr Ken Willson. He was responsible for the smooth running of the tournament and its highly detailed planning. His brief included accommodation and special catering arrangements for visiting teams and supporters, publicity, television, broadcasting and press facilities, ticket sales, interpreters, and even selecting the footballs which were to be used.

90 1966 World Cup memorabilia: the shirts worn by Roger Hunt and Wolfgang Weber in the final; the autographs of the eleven England finalists; the tournament and final programmes; a set of ticket stubs; and a stadium flag bearing the insignia of the World Cup Organisation.

Publicity was a crucial area for the WCO who were faced with the challenge of selling more than two million match tickets, which were on sale a full two years before the tournament. The WCO had no budget for newspaper advertising, and so had to find creative ways to sustain public interest during the vital build-up period, such as poster campaigns (94).

By early 1965 the WCO's official insignia was well known, and a small number of licences had been granted for its use in various forms of merchandising activity. The insignia comprised a background of the Union Flag, a circle inscribed World Championship – Jules Rimet Cup – England – 1966. It also contained a panelled football, representing the globe, with the Jules Rimet trophy and the FA coat of arms superimposed on it, designed by the commercial artist Arthur Bew. This design was to be employed for all formal and official aspects of the tournament, but was not considered appropriate for use on a wider commercial scale, and so a quest began for a more popular symbol that could be used for publicity and promotional purposes.

The FA appointed the firm of Walter Tuckwell & Associates Ltd to negotiate licences for the use of official insignia. Reginald Hoye, one of the firm's artists, produced a drawing of a small lion wearing a Union Jack soccer shirt, which met with universal popularity and was thought suitably appealing to be used on a wide range of planned merchandising.

91 A World Cup Willie lion soft toy.

The WCO's Mr Willson was a short, square-shouldered figure with a cheerfully robust and brisk manner, whose staff had nicknamed him World Cup Willie. When Mr Willson's staff first saw the stocky, amiable lion character prepared as the World Cup mascot, they detected a certain likeness to their boss. In this way the office nickname passed directly from bureaucrat to drawing, and a cartoon star and mascot was born (91).

World Cup Willie was launched in July 1965, although in a deliberately low-key manner. The occasion was the first of what were to be a regular series of press conferences at the FA's headquarters in Lancaster Gate. The primary objective was to keep journalists abreast of the competition's arrangements and update them on ticket sales figures. It was thought that newspapermen might have considered it as a gimmick if the new mascot was prominently introduced at this inaugural meeting, and so he was revealed right at the end of proceedings. However, the press were fascinated with the official mascot and within a couple of days the new cartoon star had been published in most of the leading newspapers, and later became a familiar figure in overseas journals as well. Over the following twelve months, the papers missed few opportunities to utilise Willie to

92 World Cup Willie memorabilia, including a black and white photograph of Mr Ken Willson of the WCO, after whom the mascot was named.

reflect the mood of the nation at any given time, the lion being shown in a kilt and in tears when Scotland failed to qualify for the final series.

The public relations exercise was an overwhelming success for the WCO. With awareness of the character in place, they issued almost a hundred licences authorising the use of World Cup insignia on official merchandising. As each product appeared on the high street, it had the desired effect of broadening public interest in the forthcoming competition.

For the first time the British public were exposed to an array of soccer goods and souvenirs, the overwhelming majority of the items being of an affordable and whimsical nature. A far from exhaustive listing of World Cup Willie merchandising would include such articles as souvenir cloths, reflective emblems, jigsaw puzzles, playing cards, pottery, braces, belts, balloons, plastic badges, gummed labels and car stickers, pennants, handkerchiefs, scarves, dolls, periscopes, T-shirts, hats, caps, rosettes, diaries, scrapbooks, autograph albums, calendars, confectionery, potato crisps, footballs, masks, dartboards, keyrings, slippers, glove puppets, money-boxes, horse brasses, bedspreads, bath-mats, cigarette lighters, cigars, glassware, cake decorations, towels, car badges, plaques, cufflinks and plastic figures. Additionally, Watney's, the famous brewers, produced a special World Cup Willie ale with accompanying beer glasses, and there was an official World Cup Willie song, and later a march and a waltz.

The merchandising (92) was met with great enthusiasm by the general public, and it even evoked an official World Cup Willie Collectors' Club. The financial return to the FA on the other hand, was comparatively small in the context of the whole operation, with royalties never exceeding five per cent of the net selling price, and this further helped the affordable nature of the merchandise. For the authorities, the primary objective was always to secure additional publicity, and this was achieved in spectacular fashion. The fact that England went on to win the tournament spurred interested ever further, and the merchandise craze endured well after the finals. Although much of this memorabilia is unremarkable for its quality, its celebratory connection with England's historic moment of international triumph makes it highly desirable, and such items are collected today with the same avid enthusiasm that prevailed when they were sold as new.

Collecting in this field extends far beyond World Cup Willie memorabilia. There was much official material produced for the World Cup (93), usually bearing the WCO insignia, and which of course would not have been generally available to the public. This included a number of officials' badges,

93 Official 1966 World Cup memorabilia.

identification cards, passes and other forms of accreditation; and similar items issued to pressmen and broadcasters, which also extended to clip-boards and attaché briefcases which were provided as complimentary items by the WCO.

Particularly desirable items are the lacquered gilt-metal replicas of the Jules Rimet Trophy, which were produced and presented to all FA officials in commemoration of England's victory. There is a certain amount of irony in this choice of presentation, as the FA had been highly embarrassed by the theft of the solid gold Jules Rimet Trophy, which had disappeared while on public display at the Stampex Exhibition at Central Hall, Westminster, on 20 March 1966. A week later it was discovered in the garden of a house in Beulah Hill, south-east London, by a man walking his dog Pickles. The FA made it unavailable for any further appearances before it was presented by Her Majesty The Queen to Bobby Moore after the final.

In addition to the replica trophy, commemorative sets of table mats and wine coasters were produced by both the FA and FIFA, each with colour printed depictions of the stadiums used for World Cup finals since 1930.

During the tournament, large white flags bearing the WCO insignia in the centre were flown over every stadium (90) that was hosting matches during the series, and similar designs were also used on the corner flags during the games. The insignia can also be found on the badges that were embroidered onto the blazers of players and officials, which were to be worn while they were on duty.

The WCO also produced an official handbook, which contained all the information that was essential to visiting teams, officials, journalists, and radio and television personnel. It was prepared in the four official FIFA languages of English, French, German and Spanish, and is packed with useful information, which can be of great interest to the modern collector in piecing together a historical picture. It details, for example, all the varying types of accreditation cards that were produced for different purposes; full match arrangements; a diary of all the formal and social engagements throughout the tournament; team accommodation and training venues; the teams' colours and change colours; information relevant to all the provincial towns hosting matches; and many other enlightening facts.

In addition to all these items, collectors can draw from the variety of souvenir newspapers, magazines and other publications that were brought out around the tournament, the commemorative postage stamps (dealt with elsewhere in this book), and of course match programmes and tickets.

There were two programmes produced for the World Cup (90) – the souvenir programme, covering the entire tournament, and the programme for the final between England and West Germany on 30 July. The production of both these items was fascinating, and worthy of a few words here.

Although the majority of the souvenir programme was prepared well in advance, the names of the players from the sixteen participating nations were not known until eight days before the opening match, this being the deadline stipulated by FIFA when each country's twenty-two-man squad had to be nominated. Owing to some administrative muddles there were further delays, and a complete list of the 352 players (plus photographic portraits) could not be supplied to the printers before 4 July, just seven days before England were due to play Uruguay in the tournament's curtain raiser. The printers were required to deliver the order of 1,000,000 copies by Friday 8

July in order that advance selling could begin before the opening game on the following Monday. By a magnificent feat of organisation, the printers, McCorquodale & Co. Ltd, met their deadline for the production and distribution of the forty-eight-page souvenir programme, using more than 250 tons of paper in its manufacture.

The same printers tackled the problems of the final programme with the same efficient enthusiasm. The final programme contained results, details and pictures up to and including the semi-finals, and was produced between the evening of Tuesday 26 July, when the second semi-final between England and Portugal took place and the morning of the final tie on the coming Saturday.

The ticket stubs (90) for the 1966 World Cup matches are also keenly collected. Tickets for the final were available only as part of a season ticket package for games at the host grounds of Wembley, White City, Villa Park, Hillsborough, Goodison Park, Old Trafford, Roker Park and Ayresome Park. Season tickets were issued in paper wallets containing ten, comprising of six eighth-final games, a quarter-final, a semi-final, the third and fourth place play off, and the final in any regional group area. They were also sold in multiples of seven, four and three tickets, comprising six eighth-final tickets and a quarter-final, three eighth-finals and a quarter-final, and three eighth-final matches respectively.

Last, but by no means least, any item connected directly with the England players of the World Cup final squad and the final tie, is of the utmost interest to collectors. The autographs of the England winners are highly prized, but they are surpassed in interest by any item worn or used by players during the tournament, or by medals and other awards presented to the winning team; for example, the jerseys worn by Roger Hunt and his German opponent Wolfgang Weber in the final (90). Weber had been marking Hunt during the match and furthermore scored the dramatic late goal that took the match into extra time. These jerseys were exchanged between the two players after the match.

With both England and West Germany normally wearing white international jerseys, a change of strip was necessary. England wore their red away jerseys, and first-hand sight of this kit would have been a strangely unfamiliar experience for the majority of those who watched the England side emerge from the tunnel at Wembley Stadium. Only the handful of fans who, at this period, travelled to see England playing games overseas would have witnessed the England side wearing such attire. Due to England's historic success, however, the simple, plain red shirt with the Three Lions crest embroidered over the heart, transcended from near obscurity to become one of the most remarkable and enduring images of the English game.

chapter nine

Manchester United Football Club

Many collectors, of course, concentrate on memorabilia related to the club they follow. With the phenomenal support associated with Manchester United all around the world, it is little surprise that material related to the 'Red Devils' is sought after with a conviction that has few parallels in the collecting world. Manchester United is steeped in a remarkable history, and the club has experienced widely changing fortunes. Leaner years, the drama of near bankruptcy and the devastation of the Munich air disaster have punctuated the outstanding successes achieved on the field. The ups and downs of the Manchester United story can be followed in a tangible sense by the acquisition of a wide range of memorabilia, which can cover many of the collecting fields surveyed in earlier chapters of this book.

From its origins as Newton Heath in 1878, the club entered League football in 1892–93 in the expanded First Division. The Football League had also created a new Division Two at the start of this season. Newton Heath were relegated to the Second Division in 1893–94, and these early years were a struggle both financially and on the pitch. In April 1902 Newton Heath were declared bankrupt and Manchester United was formed in its place.

Now under the stewardship of Ernest Mangnall the club began to flourish as a major force in British soccer for the first time. Mangnall brought Manchester United their first League Championship in season 1907–08, success in the inaugural FA Charity Shield of 1908, their first FA Cup win in 1908–09, and a second Championship in 1910–11, when the club's home was established at Old Trafford.

Following Mangnall's departure, and the disruption of the Great War, Manchester United's fortunes began to slide. They fluctuated between the First and Second Divisions and by the start of season 1931–32 were on the brink of bankruptcy once more. The financial rescue came from Mr James W. Gibson, a local garment manufacturer, who invested over £30,000 of his own money in the club. Under the management of Scott Duncan, Manchester United won the Second Division Championship in 1935–36, but were relegated and promoted once more before the outbreak of war.

What followed was the second great phase of the club's history. Matt Busby, a cup winner as a player with United's great rivals City, was appointed manager in February 1945. In his quarter of a century at the helm, he became

95 Manchester United memorabilia.

96 Duncan Edwards' Manchester United jersey from the 1957 FA Cup final against Aston Villa.

the most successful manager that English soccer had ever seen, and was the architect of the modern Manchester United. The club won the FA Cup for the second time in 1947–48, and three League Championships followed between 1951–52 and 1956–57. During the 1950s the young side that he had fashioned captured the imagination of the public, and the 'Busby Babes' had yet to reach their prime before tragedy struck in 1958.

Illustrated is the team line-up page in the match programme for the Red Star Belgrade v. Manchester United European Cup match on 5 February 1958 (97). It is fully autographed by the Busby Babes side. The signatures were obtained by a member of the British Diplomatic Service based in the Yugoslav capital, whose official duties included accompanying the Manchester United team to the airport the day after the match, which is where the autographs were signed. Tragically, the plane taking the team back to England crashed on take off after a refuelling stop in Munich, killing twenty-three people including eight players. These represent one of the final sets ever signed by the ill fated, legendary Manchester United team.

Busby survived the crash and, slowly but surely, began rebuilding the United side, working with a new generation of outstanding youngsters such as George Best and Nobby Stiles, and buying brilliant stars such as Paddy Crerand and Denis Law to play alongside the likes of Bobby Charlton, who had also survived the horrors of Munich. Success returned to the Manchester

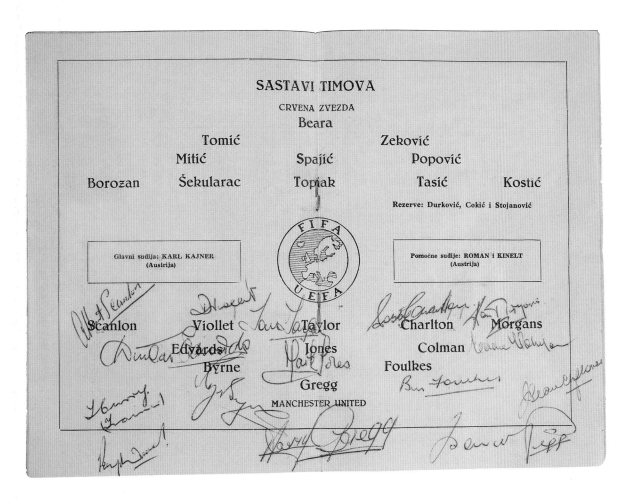

97 Red Star Belgrade v. Manchester United match programme, 5 February 1958, fully autographed by the Busby Babes on the team line-up page.

club during the 1960s, and a run of trophies that had begun with the FA Cup in 1963, followed by two League Championships in 1965 and 1967, culminated in the glittering prize of the European Cup, when United defeated Benfica 4-1 after extra time in the 1968 European Cup played at Wembley. With his ultimate ambition for the club now achieved, Busby decided to retire in June 1969, although he had to return as manager briefly when the appointment of his successor did not work out as expected. He was in fact an almost impossible act to follow. Matt Busby had been made a CBE in 1958 and was knighted ten years later.

Manchester United entered the doldrums once more in the 1970s, which included a season in the Second Division, and the decade was illuminated only by an FA Cup success under the management of Tommy Docherty in 1977. Two further Cup wins occurred (1983 and 1985) during the colourful reign of Ron Atkinson, who was responsible for the signings of many recent United heroes, most notably Bryan Robson.

The appointment of Alex Ferguson as manager in 1986 heralded the third great, and still ongoing era for Manchester United, and the 1990s have been a time of great success for the club who have proved to be the outstanding side of the decade. The elusive League honours returned to Old Trafford in 1992–93, after an absence of a quarter of a century, in the form of the new FA Premier League championship trophy, and three further championships followed. Then in truly historic circumstances, Ferguson led his team to victory in the Premier League, the FA Cup before completing a magnificent treble, when Manchester United were crowned Champions of Europe. A further championship trophy followed in season 1999–2000.

The club has fielded some of the most gifted footballers in the world in recent years, and the names of Cantona, Giggs and Beckham, to name but a few, are sure to take their place in the Manchester United hall of fame, along with the stars of yesteryear who have illuminated the history of the most famous soccer club in the world.

98 Manchester United supporters' rosettes and favours from the 1940s to the 1990s.

chapter ten

Today's Merchandise – Tomorrow's Collectables?

What was once the simple recreation of the urban working classes has now become a major industry, and a way of life for the millions who follow soccer. No other sport comes anywhere near to matching its appeal, and a culture all its own has grown up around the game.

It is an undeniable fact that in recent years soccer has attracted many new supporters from across the full range of the social-economic spectrum. For the present time at least the game is highly respectable, even fashionable. The sport's phenomenal appeal has had a profound effect on fashion, music, advertising, marketing, literature and the arts. The attraction for the business world has become overwhelming, as companies seek to market or endorse their products and services through the game's mass appeal and its roots in popular culture. For many years supporters' shops have presented collectables for sale, but in recent times the marketing of branded merchandise has mushroomed into a lucrative alternative source of income for many clubs.

As a result, the modern consumer has been tempted with an array of soccer-themed imagery and products, from which a few examples are illustrated here. What is interesting is that many of these products are not new ideas but an extension of a long tradition. A correlation can be found with older items of memorabilia highlighted in earlier chapters, and soccer, it would seem, has just been rebranded and reinterpreted for the present age. It is fascinating to compare the plastic Cadbury's chocolate container in the form of the World Cup trophy (103) with Huntley & Palmers FA Cup biscuit tin (40) of the 1920s. Gentlemen's accessories now extend to club-branded razors (100), while the proliferation of products launched to coincide with France '98 (103) has a historical background set firmly in the collectables of the 1966 World Cup. The tradition of soccer games has now entered the computer age (102).

It is impossible to predict with certainty whether future generations of collectors will be interested in the merchandise of our time, but it would be

99 A Sainsbury's point of sale poster.

surprising if they are not. The current merchandising boom is certainly indicative of the extraordinary surge of interest in soccer that has occurred in the late twentieth century, and as with all booms it surely cannot be sustained in perpetuity. Although many of these items are ephemeral in nature, the sheer scale of production in the modern age will inevitably mean that many of these items will not become scarce for a very long time. Nevertheless, a glimpse of them would seem an appropriate way of concluding this survey of over a century of soccer.

100 (below) Wilkinson Sword razors.

101 (bottom) Food and drink packaging.

102 (below) Soccer computer games.

103 (bottom) 1998 World Cup memorabilia.

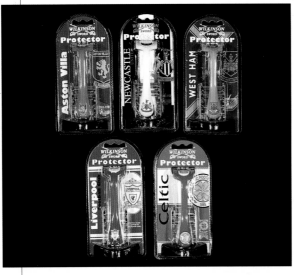

Useful Addresses

Museums

The Football Museum
Deepdale Stadium
Deepdale
Preston PR1 6RU
Opening for the millennium. Write to the above address for further details. The Museum aims to collect, preserve and interpret soccer heritage for public benefit, and to develop the finest and most significant collection of objects and associated evidence connected with the development of soccer. This will include the FIFA Museum Collection. High quality exhibitions and a range of educational and research opportunities.

The Scottish Football Museum
Hampden Park
Mount Florida
Glasgow G42 9BA
Opening: Summer 2000. Write to the above address for further details. The purpose-built site houses permanent and temporary exhibition galleries, a resources centre, including library, archive and education rooms, a collections centre with study area, a lecture theatre and other facilities. The permanent galleries examine the history of soccer and Scotland's role in its development. Extensive display of memorabilia including the collections of the Scottish Football Association and Queen's Park FC, Scotland's oldest League club.

The Manchester United Museum
Manchester United Football Club
Sir Matt Busby Way
Old Trafford
Manchester M16 0RA
Telephone: 0161 930 2904
Fax: 0161 930 2899
Web address: http://www.manutd.com
The first purpose-built club soccer museum, opened in 1986. Redeveloped in 1998 and now situated on three floors covering over 1,600 square metres of exhibition space and featuring traditional showcases, audiovisual displays and computer interactives. The museum's extensive collection of club memorabilia dates from the 1880s to the present day. There is also a club archive, open to researchers by appointment, and organised stadium tours.

The Arsenal Museum
Arsenal Stadium
Highbury
London N5 1BU
Telephone: 020 7704 4100
Fax: 020 7704 4101
Web address: http://www.arsenal.co.uk
The museum aims to promote and preserve the heritage of Arsenal Football Club. The extensive archive of memorabilia traces the history of the club since its formation by a group of munition workers in 1886, through all famous eras to the present day. The museum also features an audiovisual theatre, and organises stadium tours.

The Celtic Museum & Visitor Centre
Celtic Football Club
Celtic Park
Glasgow G40 3RE
Telephone: 0141 551 4308
Fax: 0141 551 8106
Web address: http://www.celticfc.co.uk
The museum is an integral part of the recent development and regeneration of the club. It aims to portray Celtic's heritage and capture the story of the club's growth and evolution since 1888. There are six exhibition areas exploring the complete picture of the football club, from the community and supporters to the famous players, managers and officials. The museum has an extensive collection of club memorabilia, an audiovisual theatre, and organises stadium tours.

The Liverpool Football Club Museum and Tour Centre
Liverpool Football Club
Anfield Road
Liverpool L4 0TH
Telephone: 0151 260 6677
Fax: 0151 264 0149
Web address: http://www.liverpoolfc.net
The museum houses an extensive collection of club memorabilia, including items on loan from legendary Liverpool players including Kenny Dalglish, Alan Hansen and Phil Neal, the most decorated player in British football history. State of the art interactive exhibits and a cinema-theatre complement traditional showcase displays. The museum also organises stadium tours.

Auction Houses

The following auction houses conduct special sales of football memorabilia and other auctions of sporting memorabilia

Sotheby's
34–35 New Bond Street
London W1A 2AA
Telephone: 020 7293 5000
Fax: 020 7293 5989
Web address: http://www.sothebys.com

Christie's South Kensington
85 Old Brompton Road
London SW7 3LD
Telephone: 020 7581 7611
Fax: 020 7321 3321
Web address: http://www.christies.com

Phillips
10 Salem Road
Bayswater
London
W2 4DL
Telephone: 020 7229 9090
Fax: 020 7313 2701
Web address: http://www.phillips.auctions.com

Bonhams (West Country)
Dowell Street
Honiton
Devon EX14 8LX
Telephone: 014 044 1872

Fax: 014 044 3137
Web address   http://www.bonhams.com

Brooks
81 Clapham Common Westside
London
SW4 9AY
Telephone: 020 7228 8000
Fax: 020 7585 0830
Web address: http://www.brooksauction-ers-com

Mullock Madeley
The Old Shippon
Wall-Under-Heywood
Church Stretton
Shropshire SY6 7DS
Telephone: 0169 477 1771
Fax: 0169 477 1772
Web address: http://www.mullock-made-ley.co.uk

T. Vennett-Smith
11 Nottingham Road
Gotham
Nottingham NG11 0HE
Telephone: 0115 983 0541
Fax: 0115 983 0114

Dominic Winter
The Old School
Maxwell Street
Swindon
Wiltshire SN1 5QR
Telephone: 0179 361 1340
Fax: 0179 349 1727
Web address: http://www.dominic-win-ter.co.uk

Knights
Cuckoo Cottage
Town Green
Alby
Norwich NR11 7HE
Telephone: 0126 376 8051
Fax: 0126 376 8488
Web address: http://www.knights.co.uk

Collectors' Magazines and Clubs

Programme Monthly and Football Collectable
John Lister (Editor)
46 Milton Road
Kirkcaldy
Fife KY1 1TL
Telephone: 0159 226 8718
Fax: 0159 259 5069
Published monthly. Diary of memorabilia and programme fairs, auctions and other events. News, reviews, features and advertisements including dealers, auction houses, classified and others.

The Football Programme Directory
David Stacey (Editor and Events Organiser)
66 Southend Road
Wickford
Essex SS11 8EN
Telephone/fax: 0126 873 2041
Published monthly. Diary of memorabilia and programme fairs, auctions and other events. News, reviews, features and advertisements including dealers, auction houses, classified and others. The FPD organise the International Football Memorabilia and Programme Fair at the Hotel Russell, Russell Square, London, WC1, held annually on the first Saturday in June.

The Football Collector and Historian
PO Box 29
Malton
North Yorkshire YO17 6YZ
Specialist periodical.

Sports Collector
Adwalton Publishing
14 Penfield Road
Drighlington
Bradford BD11 1ES
Published monthly. Magazine for collectors of sporting memorabilia.

Football Collector
IPC Country & Leisure Media Limited
Link House
Dingwall Avenue
Croydon
CR0 2TA
Telephone: 0208 8686 2599
A new publication. The first ever magazine dedicated to soccer collecting.

Football Card Collector Magazine
PO Box 21709
London
E14 6SR
Enquiries@footballcards.co.uk

Boot
6 Denmark Road
London N8 0DZ
Published monthly. Concentrates solely on advertisements for soccer collectables.

Winger
200 Bradford Road
Otley
West Yorkshire
LS21 3LT
Telephone/fax: 0194 346 7967
Published monthly. General football interest, including auction news and reports, and classified advertisements.

Association of Football Badge Collectors
Keith Wilkinson (Secretary)
18 Hinton Street
Fairfield
Liverpool L6 3AR

The Football Postcard Collectors Club
Bryan Horsnell (Hon. P.R.O.)
275 Overdown Road
Tilehurst
Reading RG31 6NX

UK Programme Collectors' Club
John Litster (Secretary)
46 Milton Road
Kirkcaldy
Fife KY1 1TL

Association of Football Statisticians
Ray Spiller (Secretary)
22 Bretons
Basildon
Essex SS15 5BY